Foste

A Child's Unique Story of courage, determination and perseverance

By DeJay Lester

Dedication

In dedication to my book, I would like to dedicate this book to my daughter Olivia. My love for you continues to grow as each day passes. Every day I work harder than the day before as I strive to give you the phenomenal life you deserve. When I first laid eyes on you that September day I knew you would change my life. In such a short period of time, you've taught me how to find love and joy in my heart.

I'd also like to dedicate this book to both of my mothers' Zipporah Abutu and Owillender Lester. On several occasions these beautiful women have motivated me, pushed me, encouraged and inspired me to become who I am today. I am thankful they taught me the important knowledge that was instilled in them.

Table of Contents

Acknowledgements

Everyone's life contains an untold story. When the idea approached me to compose a book to share my untold story, I wasn't aware of what I was getting myself into. The time and effort I put into making this book extraordinary was extensive but all too rewarding. Writing this book was an emotion yet freeing experience for myself, especially after holding negative feelings inside for all these years. I hope you enjoy reading this book as much as I enjoyed composing it. I truly hope that those who read this book are motivated and inspired by the experiences shared and the lessons that can be learned. To those who are battling similar situations in foster care or whom adopted foster children, if you dare to dream, every situation can and will have a positive outcome. Remind yourself how courage is special and you are deserving. Be willing to understand that world, nor the people in it, are going to change for you, so be ready to bend and change for whatever life throws your way. While you're finding your way, remember there is nothing in life you can't handle.

I would like to thank my family, friends, teachers, mentors, teammates, coaches, and Jared Easley. Thank you for believing in me and pushing me in the right direction throughout the years. With their help I was able to set goals and accomplish dreams, like writing this book for you. Thank you!

Chapter 1
Scars

MY DAD CLOSED the front door in the police officer's face and sent me to my bedroom to put my stuff away. I set my backpack down on my twin-sized bed and walked back toward the living room.

As soon as I re-entered the room, my father hit me with a bamboo stick.

"Stop!" I shouted. "What are you doing?" I ran from my father as he chased after me in a strange version of cat-and-mouse. My father threw things at me and called me a "black ungrateful bastard."

The police officer that had been standing at the door just moments before was pounding on the door demanding to see me. He threatened to knock the door down if my father didn't open it.

My father saw that I was bleeding, so he sent me to the shower before finally allowing the officer into the apartment. I overheard my father telling the officer that nothing was wrong despite the officer's insistence on seeing me before he left. My father had ordered me to my room and told me to stay there, and I complied because I was terrified of what he might do to me.

My father spent the next 10 minutes arguing with the officer before another officer arrived, at which point my father eventually agreed to let them examine me. When I returned to the kitchen wrapped only in a towel, all eyes were on me. One of the officers said he heard me screaming, and he asked me what happened. They seemed truly concerned about my safety, but I could only think of what my father would do to me after the officers left.

I wanted to tell them everything that had happened, but instead I told them that I hurt my foot and that I was yelling as a result of the pain.

The officers left me with my father that night, but they reported the incident to the Department of Child and Family Services. I knew, though, there was another beating coming.

My dad slapped me several times that night and warned me against having the woman from school call him again. I agreed between sobs, and went to my room and cried myself to sleep.

That night was one of many times I covered for my father.

The next day, I walked to school with my neighbors as usual. I was still haunted by the fear of what would happen if the school called my father again.

When my name was called over the school intercom later that morning, my mind raced. *What had I done? Why was I being called to the principal's office?*

When I got to the principal's office, there was a woman with an official-looking nametag waiting for me, along with other people from the school.

Looking back, it makes sense that the school got involved since the whole incident started at school, after all.

NINE DAYS EARLIER, on February 8, I was late leaving the after-school program because one of the counselors had noticed the scars covering my body. She questioned me about the scars, but I blamed them on the jungle-gym. I refused to admit anything to her.

Since I was busy meeting with the counselor, my neighbors walked home without me, which meant I had to make the 10-block trip alone. And I was terrified. Rude people drove past me yelling vulgar things, so I hid in the bushes along the sidewalk to escape their attention. When I stopped to look for my house key, a truckload of drunk people pulled up beside me and called me the n-word and threw beer cans at me.

I got scared and ran back toward the school and told one of the teachers there that I had lost my house key. The teacher tried to call my father to explain what had happened and to arrange for him to pick me up, but he didn't answer. She tried several more times to call him, but it was almost 7 p.m. when my father finally answered his phone. Despite her request that he pick me up from school, he insisted that I could walk home alone. Furthermore, he said, the apartment manager could open the door for me once I got there. The teacher urged him to pick me up from school, but he said he wasn't going to come get me and he said I should "walk my black ungrateful ass home." She refused to let me walk home and demanded that my father come get me. She told him that, if he refused, I would be reported to the police as an abandoned child.

The police department sent an officer to the school, and the officer also called my father at work. My dad yelled at the officer and repeatedly called me a "bastard," at which point the officer loaded me into his car and took me to our apartment. I knew from the tone of my father's voice on the telephone that I was going to be in big trouble when I got home.

As soon as we got to the front door, my father yanked me into the apartment and tried to shut the door in the officer's face. The officer warned my father to be careful about how he treated me, but my dad assured him that Nigerian culture allowed him to discipline me any way he pleased. The officer also told him that he needed to take better care of me and pick me up the next time the school called, but my father continued to argue.

And then my father closed the door in the officer's face, and sent me to put down my backpack.

THE CASEWORKER ASKED me what happened that night at the apartment. She asked me why my father wouldn't come pick me up from school that day. Then she asked me if my father hit me. I assured her that he didn't, and that I had simply stubbed my toe.

At that point, another caseworker came into the room and asked if they could look at my body and at my scars.

"If you're afraid of him, just tell me that," she said. "Help us help you."

They took me to another room and asked me to remove my clothes so they could examine my scars. The caseworker asked me repeatedly how I got the scars, but I told her that they were from earlier times when I fell.

I knew she wasn't buying my lies, but I also knew that if my dad found out I had admitted to anything, it wouldn't be good for me. I was terrified of the personal questions she was asking me, and even more afraid of what they would do with the information.

At the same time, though, I felt safe with her. She told me that I didn't have to lie anymore, and she told me that what my father was doing to me was wrong. She assured me that I didn't deserve to be treated that way. While she was talking, an image of my mother came to mind, and I could feel tears running down my cheeks.

The caseworker told me that I would have to make a grown-up decision that would affect me tremendously for the rest of my life. She offered me a choice to be happy or be abused. I finally had the opportunity to choose to be happy: to play with toys and do fun things that all little boys should enjoy. She told me she could break me free from the chains that were weighing me down for so long.

In that moment, I gave up protecting my father. I broke down and told her everything about my scars and how I accumulated them. I told her how my dad would lock me in my room if I told anyone a single thing. I told her how he hit me with different objects on my face, legs, arms, and anywhere else he could find that would hurt. I told her how I was told to keep my mouth shut about the night of February 8th. I also told her that on my birthday, December 14th, I was beaten. And I told her my father called me hurtful and demeaning names like "bastard," "stupid," and "idiot."

After I confided in the caseworker, I felt like a traitor. I felt a sense of shame that I had betrayed my father by telling a secret I kept for so many years. My counselors reassured me that I should not feel any guilt for the awful things my dad did to me. They said I was a brave little boy who deserved to be happy. They told me they saw great potential and success in my future.

That same day, DCFS also interviewed my father. Shockingly, he admitted to disciplining me but he didn't admit to abusing me. He blamed the scars on other things and insisted they were not from him. He also said he didn't care if I was taken away from him.

Later that day, when I got to the after-school program, I was told I wouldn't be going back to my father's home. I was going to a shelter home, which was a temporary arrangement: a transition between leaving the abusive home and finding a new home.

Although part of me felt relieved, I started to regret telling her the things my father put me through. I also feared that I would never see my mother or my biological family ever again. Despite my fear, I told her how crazy my father really was, and I feared he was somewhere out there trying to find me and take me back home. She assured me that would never happen and that I was going to be okay.

It felt good getting out the situation I endured for so long, but I still felt that I had abandoned my family. Even though it hurt, I knew I was being raised in a violent and neglectful house when I stayed with my father. He was never there for me, and he was never home; he was always at work or out doing other things.

The only thing I had ever wanted from him was his time.

Chapter 2
Scraps

I WAS BORN in Columbus, Ohio in 1988, but I only lived in the United States for a few years. My mother was in the United States on a visa, and my father was attending school at The Ohio State University. When my mom's visa expired, she returned to Nigeria to be near her family, taking me with her. I spent the next several years living in Nigeria, learning the languages and immersed in the culture. I was with my mom, and life was good.

In 1996, my father traveled to Nigeria with my 9-year-old half-sister Jerusha, except that I didn't know she was related to me. He was there to marry my mother, although it was really more like a renewal of vows since I was 7 years old by that time. What I didn't know at the time was that my father believed that my birth had been a mistake. And his mother believed that my mom was trying to take my father away from her.

During the reception, my mother and father danced together as the wedding guests watched and threw money at them in keeping with local tradition. While they were dancing, a woman approached and wiped a white handkerchief across my mother's face. Within minutes, a rumor circulated that my father had enlisted someone to cast a voodoo spell on my mother. When I heard the rumor, I ran to see my mother, but she said she didn't feel well. She complained of pain in her face, and I noticed a scar on the left side of her face that hadn't been there before.

My father returned to the states after the wedding, leaving my mom and me behind. My mother was in constant pain, and she kept getting weaker. She spent much of her time seeing specialists in an attempt to regain her health, but nothing ever worked. I could see the weakness in my mother, for she was not herself at all. She asked my father to bring her to the states so she could see American doctors, but he refused.

TWO YEARS LATER, in 1998, my father's brother Abraham approached my mom about sending me back to the states to be with my father. My mom was opposed to the idea at first, but my dad pushed and argued until my family agreed to let me go.

One day, when I returned home after playing with friends, my mom sat me down and told me that I needed to go live with my father.

"I'm not going anywhere," I told her. I fought with her, but she insisted that I needed to go because the opportunities would be better there. I ran off so that they couldn't make me go with my uncle. I went to my best friend's house because I didn't know where else to go. Eventually, though, his mom took me back home, and I cried because I knew that I would be leaving Nigeria, and my mom.

As the days continued, I became angrier about leaving my mother and family behind, but I didn't know what to do about it. Every night I had dreams about leaving. It was frustrating, too, that I had no say in whether I would stay or go.

On May 17, 1998, when I was 9 years old, I returned to the United States, and it was one of the scariest things I have ever done. I didn't know when I would see my mother again, and I was going to live with a man that I hardly knew. My uncle Abraham took me to the airport and the flight attendants helped me get through security and get to my terminal.

The 20-hour trip was terrifying because my only experience on an airplane had been as an infant, and I didn't remember any of it. We talked about airplanes a lot in Nigeria, but we didn't know anything about them. I was terrified that I was going to drop through the bottom of the airplane, and I had a death grip on the seat through much of the flight. The flight attendants gave me earphones and tried to keep me busy, but I didn't know how to work any of it because it was all new to me. I had grown up making toys out of scraps of straw and animal skin, so I had never seen anything like this. Eventually I fell asleep as I made the 20-hour trip to Salt Lake City, Utah, alone.

When my plane arrived at the airport, my father wasn't there. He sent his girlfriend, Lori, whom I had never met before, to pick me up instead, because he was working. Lori took me to McDonalds to get something to eat, and then she took me to the

Deseret Industries in Ogden, Utah, and bought me some toys, including a GameBoy device with games. But when she was ready to leave, I threw a fit because I didn't want to go. I was completely amazed by the things they had in the store because I had never seen anything like it.

It was all overwhelming. I was accustomed to organic, natural food that grew around my complex in Nigeria. And I grew up playing with slingshots and making toys out of whatever scraps we could find. I had never eaten this kind of food or played with electronics. And though it should have been exciting, I was completely lost. I didn't know the language, and I didn't know what to say to this lady. I didn't even know how to introduce myself.

Lori took me to her apartment, because my dad was working, and she took care of me there. After a few days passed without me seeing my father, I was frustrated and confused. I thought I was coming here to spend time with him. There were many strange people in and out of Lori's house and there was always chaos there. She did eventually take me to see my dad at his workplace, and we visited for a while and then returned to her apartment.

After several weeks passed, I did go live with my father in his apartment in Ogden, Utah. My father enrolled me in the 4th grade at Dee Elementary School, and Lori left him soon after. I had no one to take care of me, and my father sometimes would not come home, or even leave money for me. I also had no idea how to cook or what to cook, so I ate graham crackers and milk for dinner every night, or whatever I could find in the house.

Sometimes he left me at his ex-wife's house with my half-sisters while he was out doing what he was doing. (My father kept his ex-wife Ruth Mamman and my mother a secret from one another for years until they discovered the truth about one another.) Even there, I never had a real cooked meal to eat or anything to do.

The nights my father *was* home, he treated me like I was a piece of trash. He beat me, threw things at me, spit on me, and basically did anything he wanted to do. At times, he invited my half-sisters over, and he treated them like angels while he made me do things like wash the dishes and clean what everyone else dirtied. I never had fun doing anything. I always stayed in the house all day on the weekends because my father was never home.

As school continued, I finally met some Hispanic kids from school who lived next door. When my father was away, they invited me over to hang out. We played soccer on the Playstation system and we played card games. When my father signed me up for soccer, my neighbors were on the same team. Soccer proved to be a great thing for me because I was surprisingly good at it. It also gave me an opportunity to release my pent-up frustration, and I wasn't as angry when I was playing soccer.

Those friends moved away, but I eventually met another friend who walked home from the after-school program with me because he lived about 2 blocks away. We had water fights and hung out, but it never lasted long, and I always had to head back to my father's apartment.

Back to the apartment where my father slammed the door on the police officer. Back to the apartment where my father hit me in the face. Back to the last apartment I would share with my father before I found my way into the shelter.

Chapter 3
Hungry

ALTHOUGH I WAS glad to be free from my father, I still always felt that I had abandoned and betrayed my family. Even though it hurt, I knew I was being raised in a violent and neglectful house when I stayed with my father. He was never there for me, and he was always at work or out doing other things.

But shelter life wasn't good, either. I didn't feel safer staying there, because I worried that my sperm donor was going to find me and make me go home with him.

The longer I stayed in the shelter, the more I started to dislike it. I hated the routine and the monotony of the days: eat breakfast, go to school, return from school, have some fun time, go to bed. Plus, I wasn't comfortable in the clothes they gave me, but I had to manage. We couldn't wear our regular clothes; we had to wear the clothes they handed out to us.

With everything that had happened, many nights I cried myself to sleep from nightmares of what my father would do to me if he came and took me away. I even had nightmares so extreme that I would wake up in the middle of the night drenched in sweat, haunted by the years of abuse. I had nightmares of people grabbing me in my sleep, so I would curl up into a ball and rock back and forth on my bed.

Allie, however, was the bright spot at the shelter. She taught me how to play basketball, and she took me out each day to shoot hoops. As she watched me play, she told me that I was going to be something special. Allie made me promise that I would never forget about her, and I always stayed true to that promise. As time went on, I started trusting Allie more and more. She taught me new card tricks and played board games with me.

I stayed in the shelter for a while until my counselor found a home for me in Washington Terrace. Things started out okay, but as time progressed, things deteriorated. The family removed me from Dee Elementary during 6th grade and placed me in Washington Terrace Elementary. Because they never fed me, I consistently complained about being hungry to the new family. The father in the new family always got angry at me for saying I was hungry. The only thing I was allowed to eat was grilled cheese sandwiches.

One day, he made his daughter angry and she wrote "I AM HUNGRY" on the laundry room wall. (I later found out that she intended to write, "I AM ANGRY.") Her father came toward me yelling and fussing at me, rambling about the writing on the wall. I repeatedly told him that I had nothing to do with the writing on the wall, but he kept calling me a liar and saying I was a piece of shit for doing the bad deed. The mother of the family pleaded with him to calm down while she tried to get to the bottom of the situation.

In the middle of all the activity, the daughter came home and questioned what was going on inside. The parents led her to where "I AM HUNGRY" was written on the wall, and she confessed that she was the one who had written it. After her confession, the father took her to another room and yelled at her.

There was also another African-American foster child being raised in the same home, and he and I shared a room downstairs. Like boys sometimes do, he and I wrestled with each other, until one day he was trying to touch me inappropriately, so I stopped playing with him altogether.

Because we shared a room, I couldn't avoid all interactions with him, and one night, as we were lying down to go to bed, he came over to the side of my bed and tried to kiss me. I pushed him off of me, and the mother came in because of the commotion. She saw what was happening and called my counselor. The next day I was removed from the home and placed back in the children's shelter.

After about a week at the shelter, I was placed in a new home with an older Caucasian lady at her home in Ogden. She used to work at a group home, and she gave me the best care I'd had thus far. I found myself constantly doing things by myself while she was away at work, but eventually I met some friends across the street and hung out with them when I had nothing else to do.

Through everything, I missed my mother the most. I missed her more than anything in this world. My mom always made me feel safe and secure. I never felt alone while I was with her, and I found myself constantly dreaming about her smile. I was a lost boy who came to live with a man who hardly saw any of my childhood; a man who took me away from my mother. Nights like these, I cherished sleeping next to my mom in her warm embrace. She knew just the things to do to make me sleep peacefully.

But I had to go with the flow of this emotional rollercoaster and stayed in the shelter until another home was found.

Chapter 4
Profanity

DURING MY STAY in Ogden, a family named the Lesters came to visit the lady I was staying with, but I thought they were friends of my guardian at the time.

The family sat in the living room discussing my story through the foster care system, and I sat near Mrs. Lester playing with my toy car. I was very shy and quiet toward them as they talked with my caseworker and guardian. Mrs. Lester heard my story and wanted to bring me home. I didn't say much during the visit, because I was shy, but I've never had a feeling like I had that day. She had such a soft voice and I had an instant connection to her.

After about 45 minutes, we said goodbye to each other and I told them it was nice meeting them. As the Lesters left that day, I had a comforting feeling about Mrs. Owillender Lester that I hadn't felt in the foster care system up until that point. She had such a soft, unique voice that I actually paid attention to her. I ran to the door and peeked outside as the Lesters climbed into their green van, and Mrs. Lester caught me peeking at her.

Soon after the visit, my caseworker told me that the lady I was staying with was going to be moving out of state, and in February of 1990, I moved into the Lesters' home.

I was just starting the 5th grade, and I was struggling with my academics. While I was enrolled at Sunset Elementary, I drew attention from all my peers and teachers because it seemed as if I was the only black student on campus. It seemed that being African-American landed me a seat in the back corner of the classroom so I couldn't participate in any classroom activities.

Kids on campus called me different names at recess, so I resorted to fighting with my classmates when they teased me. My classmates called me names like "Useless," "Darkness," "Blacky," "Stupid," "Retard" and other demeaning and hurtful names, so I fought them for the fun of it.

One day when I was in class, I noticed some of my classmates were playing with Pokémon cards even though they were banned from school premises. I went into the classroom and told them that I was going to tell on them, and then walked out to recess. After recess, I re-entered the classroom, but before I had the chance to breathe, I was called into the principal's office.

The principal claimed that I used profanity when I spoke to my classmates. She never asked for my side of the story. She just kept telling me I was wrong, and she kept saying she believed the other kids. I didn't even know what the word "profanity" meant, nor had I ever heard the word. Even though my father called me names using profanity, I didn't know the definition of the word. The school called my adoptive dad and expelled me. As we were leaving campus, the same kids laughed at me and teased me and called me "stupid." When I ran to go fight them, my adoptive father told me to stop.

After being expelled from Sunset Elementary, I was placed in Hill Field Elementary for the remainder of the 5th grade school year. The transition made things slightly better, but school was still rocky at times. I still wound up in many different altercations at my new school. In one incident, a kid ran his mouth to me so I shoved him to the ground. His mother was present and she threatened to call the police. As a result of the incident, I was suspended again.

When I retuned to school, I had a meeting with the principal and a woman named Teresa Flenniken, who founded a program for students who were struggling in school. She watched my eyes dart back and forth from the principal to her as I tried to assess the situation I was in. As a child who was as severely traumatized, I came to the conclusion that adults could not be trusted and I had to step up and fight for myself because no one else would. Teresa suggested I could take part in her program immediately.

Teresa's program was called the CASIE program: Creating Alternative Strategies in Education. The CASIE program was created for children and kids who struggled in school but didn't necessarily fit into the Special Education program. The CASIE program was more diverse than the Special Education program because, although these kids were behind in school, it wasn't because of lower IQs or learning disabilities. Kids in this program were showing signs of extreme behavioral swings, but not as a result of emotional or mental illness. The program was designed to help kids who were struggling because of the circumstances of their environments. Mrs. Flenniken spent time with the struggling students in a secluded classroom until we showed enough behavioral progress and could proceed back to normal classrooms.

Once I entered the program, her first job was to earn my trust, which wasn't easy. She told me she was compassionate but not sympathetic for struggling students. She believed that one's success came from being held to the same standards as everyone else, regardless of your challenges. She mentioned that patience and unconditional acceptance were important factors to having a high self-esteem. She taught me not to lower my expectations. After a short time, I caught on remarkably fast with her help and the help of my foster parents.

I can remember the pivotal moment when I understood that I was in control of my own actions. Like before, I was in trouble on the playground, and Teresa asked me why I thought I was in trouble.

"Because I'm black," I mumbled while looking down at my feet.

"Do you know John?" she asked, pointing to the most popular boy in school.

"Yeah," I mumbled forcibly.

"You know he gets almost straight A's, he is the president of the 6th grade, and all the girls like him. Right?" she asked.

"Yeah," I whispered.

"What color is John?" she asked.

"Black," I muttered.

"If you want what John has, you have to do what he does," she said.

At that moment, she knew her words had sunk in by the look in my eyes. I could tell by her facial expressions that she was excited. For the first time, she knew I was making progress and she knew she had finally gotten through to me.

I finally understood the two major points she was trying

to get across to me: Adults can be trusted and I have the power to make my own life better. After that lecture, I began to trust her and follow her guidance.

As my 5th grade year ended, I moved to Clinton Elementary to begin the 6th grade school year. This school had fairly good teachers, Mrs. Jemmett being one of them. Unfortunately, I still stumbled into problems at this school, too.

During the school year, I was put into a city football league. I played running back, defensive end and kicker for the Sunset Eagles. We had a dominant year; we won every regular season game. After the regular season was over, I got sick and couldn't make it to practice, and the team lost in the first round of playoffs. Even though it was a disappointing end to the season, we still had an overall good year. I was also competing in the Jr. Jazz basketball league and I had a nice season there as well.

Mrs. Owillender went out of her way to make sure I had everything I needed and more. We attended True Vine Baptist Church together, which is where I first met Bobby Porter. Bobby had a son named BJ who happened to be my age. I also met Mike Thompson, Mateo Lacey, and their families while attending church. Given the emotional rollercoaster I was riding, I had the tendency to become explosive at the slightest conflict. This anger came from all the disciplinary actions I faced in the school system, especially all the transition between schools. Every school year seemed as if I was being transferred to another whole new world.

The Lesters, it turns out, were a Godsend. Mrs. Owillender was different. The feeling was different. She made me feel wanted and appreciated for the first time in foster care. She didn't make it about the money but about me as an individual. For the first time, I finally felt loved and wanted by my new family.

Chapter 5
Survival

WHEN I WAS a young boy, I thought that my father and I were doing ok, despite the fact that we fought every day. What I didn't realize, though, was that the daily abuse was causing me to develop anger issues. I didn't realize that, had I stayed with my biological father, one of us would have done something we regretted due to all the anger between us.

I am forever and eternally grateful to the foster care system. Although the foster care system is not perfect and never will be, it showed me how other families lived and what their daily lives looked like. Foster care won't solve every situation, but it showed me that I had the potential to improve my situation. It taught me that I didn't have to listen to my father always putting me down, or abusing me.

Although I was not in favor of being taken away from my biological family, foster care became not only an escape from my current situation but a whole new experience. As I got older, even though I constantly thought about my real family, it felt good to be loved and treated as human being and not an animal

Being in foster care requires resiliency, because going home to home and not knowing what tomorrow will bring can be a very difficult thing. I found it hard to adjust at times, because I was moving into a complete stranger's home. I wondered if they would like me, and whether I would like them. I wondered if I would get to see my other family? And I wondered if they would abuse me. And the list goes on and on.

At times, foster care was frustrating. But the thing I've learned about it is that you have to adapt and not give up. Being a foster child taught me to adapt at an early age. It taught me to be resilient and to focus on important things. While other kids worried about playing and toys, I worried about survival. Would I fit in? Would I be liked? Could I trust anyone?

At the end of the day, foster homes were a mixed bag. I learned a lot, but I am happy the whole experience is over. Having to adapt to new family rules and standards every few week or months was a hassle. Every family is really different and you never fully feel settled. Something that is acceptable in one house can be outlawed in another, which can lead to them labeling you as a "bad kid." When this occurs, the fingers start pointing when something goes missing in a home. Some families, too, would pretend all was good when your social worker came around but then wouldn't give two sh*** about you when your social worker wasn't around.

I've learned not to wait for a silver spoon to be handed to me but to rely on myself by working for everything I want in life. Instead of allowing my dark past to hinder my success, I was able to mature at a very young age and see things most adults have yet to see because people my age are focused on partying.

So many people have different perceptions of the foster care program. Some ridicule the system and some are in favor of it. I was a success story for the foster care system.

My foster family, the Lesters, made me the person I am today. They taught me how to walk, talk, and act like a normal child, while assuring me that I was worthy and that I could overcome any challenge that life had to offer. They took me into their home and transformed me from a young, terrified, and abused child into a kind, genuine, hard working gentleman. I have to say I owe each and every day of my life to them because of all they did for me in order for me to be successful.

Chapter 6
Sports

AROUND MY 6TH grade year, my natural father coordinated plans with his sister Charity to gain visitation rights. On July 10, 2001, the court agreed to expand visitation rights with my Aunt Charity. Personally, I disliked visiting her because she never took advantage of the rights given to her. Honestly, no one knew what her real intentions were. Most of the time she would pick me up and leave me at my half-sister's house while she spent her time elsewhere doing people's hair or visiting her boyfriend.

My half-sister and I shared the same father but had different mothers. She never showed interest in any of my activities like football or school. While I was at her apartment during a visit, she mentioned to me that I needed to go back to my father and she said I was an ungrateful child. She called me an "ungrateful bastard." As she pressed on, I walked out of her apartment and went to the neighbor's apartment. The neighbor allowed me to use the phone to call my adoptive parents and tell them about what was taking place. They came and picked me up, and a couple of days later, a court hearing was held that terminated my Aunt Charity's visitation rights.

Around that time, my adoptive mother decided that she wanted to send me to a school named Salt Lake Christian Academy. She consulted Coach Bobby Porter about the transition and he recommended it. He said that it would be a good idea for me to attend Salt Lake Christian Academy because private schools have smaller class sizes. The year I was supposed to attend Salt Lake Christian Academy, however, the school closed down. Bobby Porter and his family moved to Layton, Utah, and he suggested I attend Layton Christian Academy.

When I began Layton Christian Academy, I was a rough 7th grader who didn't know right from wrong. I didn't know who was for me or against me either. I struggled with my academics and I struggled to control my temper. I never wanted to be in school or class.

The smaller Christian school brought positivity into my

life, but I was still convinced that everyone was against me. At first, my only friend was Mr. Porter. As time progressed, I began to trust Mr. Martin and Mrs. Elmy. They always devoted time to talk to me when I got into trouble and they reminded me that they truly cared about me. Through their guidance, I learned there was a more constructive way to solve problems other than fighting. My grades and temper improved as a result of their counseling.

Mrs. Owillender Lester enabled me to thrive as a young teenager. As things improved, I learned about creating a positive relationship with God. With the help of Mrs. Owillender and Coach Porter, I turned my life over to Christ. I let God guide my life from that moment on. I quit blaming God for my misfortunes and began to realize how blessed I really was.

In September, we moved into another home, and we changed churches. As time went by, I met Shawn Washington and his family at Second Baptist Church. The more time Shawn and I spent together, we started to have a brother relationship. We constantly spent the night at each other's houses, and we served as ushers together at our church. Shawn and I spent a lot of time together.

After getting settled into our new home, I played basketball from dawn until dusk. I loved basketball so much that it became my number one sport in no time. After the move, I still attended the scrimmages that were held at the Clearfield Job Corps. Coach Porter put together a basketball team for us. I met Jerrell Stewart and a couple of other kids on the basketball team. I often joined BJ and his friends, Mike Thompson and Mateo Lacey, playing basketball with high school kids at Job Corps. We lifted weights, ran, and practiced before scrimmaging.

I eventually figured out that Jerrell lived a couple blocks from me, so I caught rides to school and to Clearfield with him. He became a best friend to me and we hung out regularly. Basketball became my safe haven when things were rough.

Around this same time, Mrs. Owillender was diagnosed with a disease called Scleroderma. Scleroderma is a chronic autoimmune disease that causes water to build up around the heart. As the disease worsened, it affected her legs, making them swell to the point that she was immobile. The disease also caused sharp pains in her arms, and it caused a large buildup of mucus in her lungs. Despite all of the hardships, she was a true soldier. She always went out of her way to make sure the family was doing well.

For Mrs. Owillender's treatment, she had two oxygen tanks: one for when she left home and the other for when she was home. She was also given a machine that hooked up to her heart. This machine had a cassette that you had to make by mixing two medications together. After the two medications were mixed together, the mixture was put into the cassette and placed in the refrigerator. When one cassette ran out, she would have to refill a new one and change it on a regular basis.

Despite having to get up early for school, I stayed up late at night to talk to her about everything from school to relationships, and I cooked for her when she was hungry. Sometimes I look back and think I took those days for granted. For the first time in my life, I felt loved and I felt like this was where I belonged. I felt like I had a second mother and I had someone that could understand where I was coming from. I also knew that she cared for me and was not just using me.

With this in mind, I also spent a lot of time thinking about my biological mother. I wondered when I would be able to see her again. I always dreamed of her soft touch and cuddling up next to her when I was scared or felt lonely. I opened up to my adopted mother Mrs. Owillender more every night about my life story. She was fascinated by my story and she was always interested in what I was telling her. She told me that she was glad she was able to bring me into her home.

As I became more involved in sports, she tried her hardest to make it to as many games as possible. She became my biggest supporter and my biggest fan. I loved every minute of her involvement. My most cherished memory was playing basketball against our rivals my freshman year in high school.

The score was tied and we had the ball running a played we called stack high. Jerrell had the ball in the middle of the court by half court. I was on the left wing above the 3-point line. With about 10 seconds left, Jerrell made a move to the basket.

While driving to the basket, he went up for the layup on the right side of the basket. I made my way toward the basket on the left side just in case he missed. He was bumped, but no foul was called. The ball stayed on the rim before it came off the rim on the left side. I remember glancing in the stands for a quick moment and seeing Mrs. Owillender gaze at me with excitement.

I jumped in the air and grabbed the ball in mid air. The whole gym went quiet and all I had was tunnel vision. I hung in the air and time seemed to stop. I let the ball go off the glass, and the ball went into the basket as the horn sounded. My teammates went crazy and the whole gym erupted. The celebration began and all I could think of was Mrs. Owillender and the smile she had on her face as she watched me make the game-winning shot. I had never felt anything like that since my younger years with my biological mother.

In 7th grade, we had three basketball teams. We had an A, B, and C team. Although I felt like I was good enough to play on the A team, I was placed on the B team for most of the year, but I played on the A team for some special occasions. In 7th grade, I also started playing soccer. I played middle forward and goalie, and I also ran cross-country and played baseball.

In my 7th grade year, I was immature and did a lot of dumb things. I remember putting Vaseline on a girl's locker handle so she couldn't open it. I also argued with many people just for my enjoyment. I had a childhood crush but I could never find a way to approach her or ask her out. Every time I interacted with her, I was mean to her or I did something stupid to try to get her attention. My crush for her carried on into the next year.

My 8th grade year was better for me as both a student and as an individual. In basketball, we won the Christ Classic, a championship tournament in Salt Lake City. We also had an undefeated season, and our team beat teams by double-digit scores. That basketball season was truly one to remember. Our soccer team did well also, traveling to Pocatello, Idaho for another tournament, but we fell short. I also ran cross-country that year.

Even though sports were going great for me, my crush

agreed to go out with someone else. This destroyed my self-confidence, and I started feeling that I couldn't do anything right and no one liked me again. I carried that mentality in my head for the remainder of my 8th-grade school year. I refused to have friends at school.

In April of 2003, I was placed under permanent custody of the Lesters, and it was the best thing to happen to me. They put me in a good school that positively impacted my transition from a boy into a man. They also allowed me to play the sports offered to me where I felt comfortable. Their support helped me build and grow.

Chapter 7
Kidnapping

MY FATHER FINALLY regained his visitation rights in 2003.

He was manipulating his way through parenting classes and cooperating with the system to in order to get me back into his home. During the process, I was checked out of school numerous times to attend court hearings, and I remember the judge asking me personally if I actually wanted to visit my dad. I was scared, largely because of the haunting memories of the past, but I also missed being around my family – so I agreed to go.

"I believe in 2nd chances..." I thought to myself. "Nobody is perfect."

And who doesn't fall short? He was my father, after all. And what's a young boy without his father, right? We need fathers to teach us to be men in this world. We need our fathers to teach us confidence and self-esteem, and to demonstrate strength and leadership.

So I agreed to visit my father and stay with him for the summer and return to my foster parents at the end of the summer for school.

But my father had different plans.

I arrived in New Jersey on June 18th. I exited my plane and headed to baggage claim where my father was supposed to be waiting, but he was nowhere to be found. I scrounged up enough loose change to call him from a pay phone.

The frustration of trying to get in touch with him triggered flashbacks of him beating me for some imagined disappointment, and I wondered if I could I bear that again. I was bombarded with so many thoughts of torment and devastation.

I called my father five more times and still no answer, so I paced around the airport for some time before I went back to the pay phone and tried again. I froze when I heard his voice. All I could say was, "I'm here."

As though he'd purposely forgotten, he asked, "Where? At the airport?"

I told him I had been waiting for a while now. He said he

was on his way and I hung up the phone. Another 30 minutes passed before he arrived at the airport.

A short man came through the sliding doors, but the sun masked his face from me. I wondered if it was him, but the eerie feeling of familiarity let me know that it was. There was no emotion and no connection between us as he walked toward me. He helped me with my bags, and we rode the transit system back to his apartment in Hamilton, N.J.

My dad's apartment had one bedroom and one bathroom. The living room was divided in half by a bookshelf. Behind that was a small makeshift bedroom. There was a small mattress on the living room floor for me to sleep on, along with a lamp and a small television, which I connected my game system to. I stayed up all night playing video games and watching movies, and then I slept away most of the day. The time zone difference between Utah and New Jersey messed with my sleeping habits.

My father was never home; he was always working, and spending time with me was never his priority. He never introduced me to any of our neighbors, so I had to work to make friends. He had a girlfriend staying with him that I had never met before, and as the days passed, I didn't think much of her, either.

We didn't have a home phone, but every night, I borrowed my father's cell phone to call my foster parents and my friends from school. One night in particular, I was sitting on the porch talking to my foster-mom when my father interrupted saying he had to use the phone. I told my foster mom I would call back.

He accused me of being an "ungrateful bastard" and verbally chastised me for speaking with my foster family because, in his eyes, they weren't my family.

I tried to call my foster mother again, but she didn't answer. I handed the phone back to him, and he pretended to make a call. I say pretended because, within a minute, the phone rang. It was my foster-mom calling, but he silenced the ringer and ignored the call.

"Who was that?" I asked him.

"Nobody," he said angrily,

I again asked him if I could use the phone, but he wouldn't let me. His voice got loud and angry, and he questioned why I had to talk to my foster parents every night. He grumbled that I shouldn't have left home in the first place, clearly ignoring the fact that I was taken from this "home" due to his physical abuse. He then started another round of what an ungrateful child and a bastard I was, and I remember questioning whether I had made the right decision in returning to my father's home to stay with him for the entire summer. I've asked myself many times why my father would go through all the trouble to try to get me back, only to treat me as though I meant nothing to him.

The next night, I told my foster mother about what had happened the previous night. We sat on the phone and decided that, even though it wasn't right of him, I would be returning home to Utah soon, so it would be best to stick it out and call when I could.

Talking with my foster mother, Owillender Lester calmed me, like listening to waves crash against the sand. She had this deep wisdom that she poured into me in any given situation, and she reminded me of my biological mother. No matter what I was dealing with, she had the perfect words to kindle a fire inside me so the soft flames could chase away the darkness. Her voice could calm the ocean itself. I missed her and looked forward to the end of summer so I could go back home to her again.

Days slowly passed, most of them with my father away at work and me home alone playing video games. One morning, I woke to find all my belongings packed. As I processed what was happening, I got excited at the possibility that maybe I was going back home early.

But if the art of manipulation had a degree, my biological father had a doctorate in it. Like the serpent compelling Eve in the garden, he told me that he was taking me to see my biological mother.

It had been five years since I last felt the truest love of her embrace and four years since I had last heard her voice on the phone. Racing thoughts flooded my imagination. I was excited to return to my first true love. My mother was my heart and my world.

I have no words that can accurately or effectively describe the love I have for Zipporah Abutu, my biological mother. Who can describe the taste of water? Yet water is essential; it is life and without it, there is nothing that can live. She is water to my soul and her essence is my air. I wanted to breathe her in again and lay my ear against her chest to listen to her heart beat again. Only this could entice a child to willingly board a plane across the Atlantic Ocean.

I never comprehended that this was an evil man's ploy to kidnap me.

We had to move fast in order to catch the shuttle bus to the airport. I insisted to my father that I needed to call my foster parents and tell them that we were headed to Nigeria to see my mother, but he refused.

"No! You can do it later!"

In these moments, I had so many flashbacks of my mother and what she looked like. His angry and impatient outbursts never exposed the crime he was committing. I recalled the day I had left Nigeria to return to the United States when I was 10 years old. I recalled the last hug, the last kiss and the final good-bye to my mother.

I had lived the last five years with a suffocating loneliness that nighttime tears couldn't release. So with the excitement of a child on Christmas morning, I was about to receive the greatest gift of all – reuniting with my mother's warm embrace.

After a few minutes, the airport shuttle picked us up and made its course to the airport. I was still asking to call my foster mother, but my father kept coming up with excuses and saying his cell phone didn't work and that he didn't have any minutes. His impatience boiled under the surface, and he yelled at me and demanded I stop talking about my foster parents.

"OK," I said meekly, somewhat afraid of what he would do. I figured eventually I would find a chance to make the necessary phone call.

As we arrived at the airport I followed him to the ticket counter and through security. After security, we headed to our gate. At this point, there was nothing else on my mind but my mother's beautiful face and smile. As I entered the aircraft, I was in awe. Lost daydreams were slowly becoming a real possibility.

I hadn't seen my biological mother for six years, but I was finally getting a chance to see the woman I loved and adored. She was the love of my young life, the one who truly cared for me and protected me. At night, she dreamed her dreams beside me as I cuddled next to her in the perfect peace of a young child whose world was complete as long as she was within reach. She made sure I had everything necessary to grow up strong.

Chapter 8
Nigeria

We arrived in Abuju, Nigeria 36 hours after leaving the United States. It was stunning to see how differently everyone was dressed compared to me. The African attire reminded me of my childhood days and instantly brought back many memories and flashbacks. After exiting the plane, we headed to baggage claim but there was no sign of our bags. I followed my father to the baggage center and, after discussing the matter with airport officials, we were told we would have to wait until the next day to get our bags.

That night, I headed out to get something to eat with my natural father, his brother Abraham and my aunt Naomi from my mother's side. We went to a place that had only African dishes such as stew and rice, fufu (also known as cassava), and Fanta soda.

While we were at dinner, my family members spoke in the Nigerian native tongue. I was able to pick up bits and pieces but couldn't fully interpret everything. I hadn't spoken my native tongue since I was younger and I had already forgotten much of it from lack of use.

The following morning, after they tracked down our bags, we returned to the airport to pick them up. My Uncle Abraham chauffeured us around, and then we headed toward his home where we would stay while my father made plans for us to make the 9-hour trip to Wukari, where my grandpa and mother lived.

.

My mind was racing at the speed of light, it seemed. I was amazed that I was actually near the place where I had spent the majority of my younger life. I was finally going to see every young boy's first true love: mama. I had missed my mother with indescribable agony since the first day I was pulled from her arms to come back to the United States in 1998. I was excited to see my beloved grandfather who I cared so much about also.

It was mesmerizing to be reacquainted with life in Nigeria: the living conditions, the food, the customs and the language. My Nigerian family spoke "Jukum", our native tongue; but hearing it after so many years left me piecing together mental jigsaw puzzles, trying to recall words and place words together to create a picture of the conversations going on all around me. I hadn't spoken Jukum in so long, nor had I eaten Nigerian food. Peanut butter and jelly was as good as it got in my father's household.

But nothing brings back memories like scents and tastes, and Nigerian cuisine flooded me with flashbacks. Food here was traditionally eaten by hand. Forks and spoons, however, were becoming more common. The main thing I remember as a child was that it was considered dirty and rude to eat using your left hand.

On the third morning of waking up to tea and eggs, my Aunt Naomi and I left my Uncle Abraham's rather upscale home, by Nigerian standards, and we continued our journey towards Wukari. We left my father behind in Abuju.

We were packed like sardines along with five other people into something like a rundown old Chevy. As we got in the car, numerous street vendors ran up to the windows trying to sell the passengers oranges, bananas and other food items. We purchased some fruit and beverages for the road.

In the front row were the driver, another passenger and a fully-armed soldier to protect us from armed bandits who would often pull cars over and rob the people inside. Once the vehicle was ready to go, other soldiers standing in the street fired several shots in the air while shouting, and then we were on our way.

We rode all night packed like sardines. I remember it being incredibly dark that night. I fell asleep for the last half of the trip as we drew near to Wukari. After nearly nine hours, we entered Wukari and got out at an official stop-station.

My aunt hailed us a motorcycle taxi called an "okada." It is not unusual to see a family of six straddling the fuel tank of an okada, or even women riding with infants strapped to their backs, along with heavy luggage balanced on someone's head. Okadas navigate through traffic and ignore all traffic signs. We managed our luggage easily as our okada took us to my grandfather's compound.

My heart raced as I remembered my childhood: times I spent running around, playing with friends and playing soccer in the complex. We finally arrived at my grandpa's L-shaped home, and though the paint was peeling and it wasn't fancy, it felt like home nonetheless.

As we got off the okada I saw my aunts, uncles and cousins in the compound before they realized it was me. When they did, they got excited and ran over to us, greeting us and helping us to put our belongings away. After greeting everyone there, I questioned where my mother and grandpa were. They told me my grandpa was at a funeral. Soon, however, we were going to meet up with him.

My grandpa's complex was quite a distance from the main road, so we sent someone to hail another okada for us. The okada took us to the funeral my grandfather was attending. When he caught sight of us, his eyes filled with amazement and he was truly stunned to see me. He had aged since the last time I saw him. He was thinner and I felt sad because I felt I had missed out on so much time I could have spent with him. My grandfather and I shared an unbreakable bond. Time and distance had no effect on it. Alongside my mother, he was someone I immensely adored as he, too, held a special place in my heart.

After greeting my grandfather at the funeral, we went back to his complex. My family then discussed trip details about going to another town called Takum, which is where they said my mother was. I was very frustrated and confused wondering when I would finally see my mother.

Hours had already passed with still no sign of her. I was still piecing together conversations and listening with growing anticipation. I didn't understand why she wasn't there to be the first one to greet me. It had been years and not one moment had passed where her face left my thoughts. I spent so many lonely nights homesick for her presence, tears staining every pillow I've ever laid my head on. Nighttime fears stole my breath away, but just one simple memory of her lying beside me could send those fears fleeing.

So here I was finally – kidnapped to a world far from the past I left behind, so close to her embrace once again. Yet all these people made it feel still so far. I was growing suspicious about why everyone kept telling me she was in Takum. Why was she there and not here, at home, in Wukari?

Soon, after arrangements were made, we headed to Takum, and I was anxious to see my mother. We arrived an hour later and we stayed at my grandfather's other complex located there. We then went to the deceased elderly lady's home whose funeral my grandfather had just attended.

While we were there, my mother's family and friends told me stories about her and mused about how much I looked like my mother. I was at a boiling point about to burst into frustrated tears.

"Where is my mother?" I asked.

I firmly insisted they tell me the truth and stop playing games with me. A woman (who I assumed was an aunt I didn't know well) told me she needed me to be strong, and reminded me not to go overboard. Go overboard for what? I wondered.

Next she told me words I didn't expect or ever want to hear; words I wish I could be erased like the past. I asked for the truth but I wanted this to be a lie. She told me my mother passed away in 1999, a year after I left to live with a man who treated me worse than a neglected pet. She told me my mother died because my father refused to bring her back to the United States. That the wound and scar on her face needed to be checked out by a real doctor because it never healed and had only gotten worse.

I was flooded with memories of the party set up by my father in an attempt to get my mother back; the celebration where some woman wiped a handkerchief over my mother's face and nothing since that day was ever the same again. Flashbacks of events in a country where witchcraft was very real and a killer didn't need to be physically present to murder. This same man who killed her because he couldn't control her also tormented her with spiteful words declaring I was a mistake and an ungrateful bastard. She could not convince him to allow her back and so she stopped pressing the issue, left it alone and

45

continued living her life fatigued and still working as a nurse at the hospital in Wukari.

In the whirlwind of disbelief and heartbroken emotions, I dropped down with shattered tears and I cried like I never had before. I felt the tears falling from my eyes burning like hot lava. It seemed as if my world just turned upside down. I no longer wanted to live with the empty grief of these feelings. So many outrageous thoughts invaded my mind: thoughts about committing suicide and that I shouldn't be living here on earth without her in it; thoughts about how and what to do now without my mother? I became inconsolable as I faced the greatest loss of my life.

Losing her was the hardest thing I have ever had to endure, and knowing that she was gone forever became unimaginable.

Chapter 9

Good-Bye

DOES ANYONE EVER really get to say a "last good-bye"? And how can we know this hug will be the last time you get to feel someone else's heart beat? Who gets to decide we've had enough time to embrace the presence of those we adore and love? And how come those who seemingly don't "deserve" life seem able to indulge in it to their abundant selfish content, while the kindest and most grateful people leave too soon? How do you keep your heart warm and open enough to embrace those still living when fear of losing them wants to shut you down to avoid the pain?

I suppose everyone has regrets such as: I should have done more, been more loving, made a greater effort, and been more accepting or open minded. But we can't predict the future. My biggest regret in life is not having the opportunity to say goodbye, to hug my mother one last time or share more time with her. I want her to know surely how much she meant to me, how my sweetest dreams and memories are all of her. I'm sure a mother's last thoughts are always of her children, but I want my mother to know all my thoughts were of her.

My grandpa tried to console me, telling me I had to realize that she did not have a choice; unfortunately death was a part of life. I wanted to know where she was buried and he told me she was there, buried in his complex where he had an area that was he had not finished building yet.

My mother's death and finding out in this manner taught me a harsh lesson: we never get through life without losing someone we love, someone we need, or someone we thought was meant to be or something we assumed was meant to stay for a long time. The trials of such loss also teach strength and push us to keep moving forward in life. I also learned that I had to be greater than my circumstances.

In the end, to say that my mother was a wonderful woman is not enough. She was absolutely amazing beyond words could express inside and out. I couldn't have asked for a better mother than her. I will always love her because she was a special lady and my first true love. She always encouraged me to reach for the stars and she taught me the importance of brushing off scars by not letting things in life get me down. Most importantly, she taught me to maintain a smile no matter what. For that I am forever grateful.

Chapter 10
Vortex

Our stay in Takum lasted until after the elderly lady's burial. Nigerian funerals are different than those in the United States. Instead of mourning, it's more of a celebration of life. There's music and a huge display of honor for those who pass on and are greatly loved. A burial celebration can last a few days as family and friends come to give their respect and honor the family.

Throughout the burial celebration, I spent time with my aunts who had spent our entire time together commenting on how much I looked like my mother. And because my hair had not been cut since leaving New Jersey, they insisted I let them braid my hair in cornrows to see how much I'd resemble my mother. I agreed to their request, and when they finished, everyone stared in astonishment as if I was my mother herself looking back at them. I went to look in the mirror and as I approached it, I saw my mother looking right back at me and all I could do was cry softly. I closed my eyes so I could I remember all her facial features, from her smile to her hair.

A couple of days later we went back to my grandpa's house in Wukari. For the remainder of the summer, this was where we remained. Once we were settled there, I asked them to please show me where my mother was buried. My grandfather and I started walking toward a room in an unfinished part of the complex. That walk didn't feel real to me yet. Still we kept walking toward that room where reality finally dealt a blow that hurt to the core.

In that room was an all-white cemented grave with a white cross on top. I stood there in the silence surrounded by a surreal numbness. I didn't know what I should do as I didn't have the words to speak. Her death changed me in that moment. I couldn't feel anymore. I left my emotions there with her in that room. It was as if I left a part of my soul in this vortex and when I came back from it, there was an emptiness in my heart where hope once was.

I approached where she lay buried. A feeling came over me like she was standing next to me with her arms on my shoulder telling that everything was going to be alright. I'm not sure how long I gazed at the gravesite and that white cross. I asked God for guidance and for her to continue to watch over me. The tears that tried to fall dried up quickly as if she had wiped them away like when I was younger.

After spending this time with my mother I went and sat down next to my grandfather. We had a deep conversation about all that occurred between my mother and natural father and me. The more he told me, the more enraged I became. I want no association with this man. If I could have washed his DNA from my blood, I would have. I can't help but question how he could be so cruel and harsh towards those he was supposed to love. He destroyed a mother who was innocent and always wanted to help everyone.

Chapter 11
Superwoman

Mom,

I want to start this letter by telling you how much I love you. Every day, I am thankful to have you in my life. You were there for me every step of the way. Your perseverance helps me through the highs and lows, the ups and downs, and the rises and falls. I even remember taking my first baby steps; you fell every time I fell down.

Since I was little, you constantly held me up and never let me fall. You were the number one woman in my life, and you always will be. Ever since I was little, you were my hero, my Superwoman. Growing up was a struggle and things weren't easy for us. But despite our hardships, you always sacrificed so much to raise me. Your dedication to my well-being has meant the world to me and words cannot begin to express how grateful I am for you. You have given so much of yourself to me.

One trait I know I got from you is your strength. You have had the strength and bravery to overcome any obstacle life has put in our way. It hurts my heart that my last memory I have was you wanting to see my face again. All those years you thought you needed me. In reality, I have never needed someone so intensely as I needed you.

I cried my eyes out the day I was told I lost you. That day in 2003, I never thought my heart could hurt so badly. From that day on, there has been a broken piece of me that no one can fix. To this day, it's still hard to fathom that you're gone. I am not sure I have accepted it yet. I don't want to. There was a time I had your love and nothing else mattered. Now all I have are our memories together. You gave me fulfillment growing up, and that's the best thing I could have asked for. You brought so much joy to my life, just like I know I brought joy to yours.

I want to say thank you for everything you have done for me. Those two words mean so little compared to everything you have sacrificed, accomplished, and fulfilled for me. Thank you for always being my shoulder to cry on. When I had nightmares, thank you for comforting me and allowing me to sleep peacefully next to you. Thank you for all the laughter, smiles, life lessons, nurturing care and the unconditional love you have brought into my life. Thank you for always believing in me and reminding me that I will always have someone who loves me despite my flaws.

Throughout my childhood, you and I were inseparable. You were my 6-foot tall athletic bundle of joy. You loved playing basketball, and I know I got the passion for the sport from you. You always wore a smile on your face. You had the presence to light up any room you walked into. To this day, I think about your contagious smile, and it makes me smile. You were my favorite "hello" and my hardest "goodbye." I dreaded the day I was forced to say "goodbye" to you.

When I was sick, I remember coming to you at the hospital. Seeing you in your white nursing outfit always brought joy to my heart. You always knew exactly what to do to nurse me back to health, both at the hospital and at home. Sometimes I enjoyed coming to your work just to get your motherly hugs and to be surrounded by your presence.

Another thing I need to thank you for is the dedication you gave to others around you. When you weren't spending your time with me, you were generously spending your time helping those in need. Even when times were tough, you always managed to find a way to put a smile on someone else's face. You gave your last dollars to treat the needy instead of treating yourself. You spent your hard-earned money to buy medication for those who needed it. You found joy staying after your shift at the hospital to continue helping patients. You volunteered your time to help your co-workers instead of going home and being unproductive.

You had this presence of working for the Lord. Your patients kept smiles on their faces and never stopped fighting because they could feel God's presence through your dedication to them. Your kindness has rubbed off on me. Just like your patients, I wouldn't have made it this far without your love and guidance.

I know that all you wanted for me was success. Only God knows how many nights you stayed up praying for me to become a star or some educated success. Even with our distance, people have seen how you truly cared for me despite our lack of communication. I've heard from others that you talked about your "handsome and beloved" son until your death. You talked about wanting to see me mature from a boy into a bright young man. You wanted me to have success but stay humble while God blessed me with fortune. You dreamed of giving your only child the best wedding to a beautiful young woman, and then watching us bring grandchildren to your life. You wanted to contribute your strength, effort and money.

Mom, in your honor, I keep your words close to my heart every day. When I am feeling down, I remind myself of your dreams for me and pick myself back up. Not a day goes by that I am not reminded of your strength, and that thought fuels my fire to be better. I am continuously trying to be better for you. I know that if you were here, you would tell your prince to keep his head up because his crown might fall.

Lastly, I want to thank you for watching out for me, and helping to guide me through everyday life, and for helping me when I was in need. Thank you for being there through the difficult times and the good times. Thank you for all the amazing memories we shared together; remembering those times helped me through some of my toughest days.

Thank you for showing me what true, unconditional love really is. Thank you for your beautiful smiles and your sweet kisses. Thank you for making me smile even on my worst days. Thank you for reminding me that life is always worth living and living well. I love you and miss you. We will meet again one day, but not yet momma. Not yet.

My Mother Zipporah

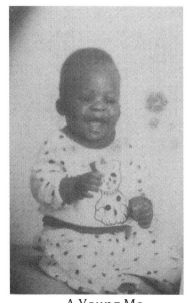

A Young Me

My Maternal Grandfather

My Mother and I

My Mom
Mrs. Lester

Accident
Dec. 12, 2008

Nigeria
2003

College Graduation

High School Football

My Little Cheerleader

Everybody Loves a Hero

My Favorite Fan

My Daughter Olivia

Chapter 12
Warrant

AS THE SUMMER came to an end, I began to worry more because I had not spoken with my natural father or heard from him at all. My father's brother, Uncle Abraham, came to visit my family and me at my grandfather's home. He came with some money that my father had sent with him. Then my uncle notified my grandfather and family that I had a warrant for my arrest in the United States, a lie created by my father. Abraham had been instructed to talk to my grandfather about me staying in Nigeria.

They sat in my grandfather's living room for hours discussing and debating this matter as I sat out front listening and waiting for them to finish. My grandfather would not budge from his decision to do the right thing and send me back; he knew what type of person my natural father was.

In truth, it was my father who had the warrant for his arrest in the United States -- for kidnapping. And yet my father was still able to fly back into the United States, taking with him my passport and all my information so it would be difficult for me to return.

My grandfather was enraged by my natural father's actions. He called me into his living room to sit me down and talk like he always did in his grandfatherly way. I opened up and told him everything: about how my father abused me physically; how he was also verbally abusive, calling me awful names; and how he was never home. I also spoke of how my foster parents took much better care of me and loved me more than he did. My grandfather told me he wasn't fond of my father and his ways and assured me we would figure out what to do from here.

As September approached, I grew anxious to return to the United States. School would be starting soon, as would football season. This was going to be my first year in high school.

My grandfather and aunt began arrangements to get me to Lagos, Nigeria, so I could to talk to my Aunt's husband who was the commissioner of police there. As plans were being made, I continued to cope with the loss of my mother.

I stayed active playing soccer in our complex with some friends and playing basketball at a local park. People questioned where I had played basketball previously, so I told them I was from America and they were all amazed by this. Everyone there has dreams about America and envisions how good it must be. My friends and I were even invited to play against the professional basketball team of Wukari. Before and after playing against the Wukari team we took pictures to have some memories.

Throughout the time I was there in Nigeria, I got to spend a lot of time with my other aunts, as well as with my Uncle Mark who was just a little bit older than me. I also went to my childhood best friend Yavala's home and spent time with him and his family, which brought back some really great memories of when we were young kids. His mother and my mother both were nurses at the hospital in Wukari. They had become best friends and were always going out of their way together to help so many other people out. His mother loved me as if I were her own and vice versa.

Chapter 13
Embassy

MY GRANDPA GATHERED all the money needed to pay for the trip to Lagos, the capital of Nigeria at that time. As our departure day came, I had one last warm grandfatherly talk with him and thanked him for everything he was doing for me. I gave him a good-bye hug and told him we would soon speak again.

My aunt and I then took an okada to get to the car that would transport us to Lagos. The car junction location was like a mini-market with vendors selling homemade foods and various fruits such as oranges, bananas and mangoes. We purchased some for the trip and packed into the car when the driver was ready for us to board. Once again we had an armored Nigerian soldier in the front seat for protection.

My aunt and I said a prayer and she rubbed some oil over my head and hers and asked God for protection. As we finished our prayer, the rest of the soldiers shouted and fired gunshots into the air, and then we were on our way.

We left at about midnight and drove all night. Because the little car also had other passengers, we were very cramped. As we drove, we passed checkpoints where soldiers patrolled the roads. They had their version of spikes on the ground - which was just a long board with nails in it. As we came to every stop the driver greeted them in the African language and gave them a few nairas' (Nigerian currency) for their services. I remember the drive to this day.

My aunt took good care of me on the trip. She kept reassuring me that she could see my mother in my eyes and that everything would be alright. At each stop along the way, people were selling everything you could think of: peeled oranges, bananas, bread, and anything you might need. After a few checkpoints, I fell asleep. When I woke up early in the morning, we were at another checkpoint in Benin City, capital of Edo State, which was south of Nigeria. We had to switch from the car to a Greyhound-style charter bus, which was run-down and nowhere near as nice as an American bus. In order to get to the bus, we should've had to take an okada to the other side of town, but since my aunt actually knew the driver of the car and offered him some extra naira, he agreed to drive us to where the buses were. We thanked him as we got all our things out and immediately went to eat some real food and brush our teeth.

As we headed to the bus, we saw a completely naked man in the street hugging the tire of a bus that was ready to depart. He was attempting to kill himself. I watched the commotion and pondered why he would want to do such a thing. Sadly, this type of thing was very common in Nigeria.

All around us, okada were everywhere, and cars were speeding left and right, dodging potholes and divots. In some places, there was no road; just dirt. It was chaos and madness, unlike anything on any American road.

We boarded the bus about 9 a.m. and again there was a Nigerian soldier with a gun in the front of the bus. We arrived in Lagos later that evening. Once we made it to the bus stop, we had to switch vehicles again, but this time it was a taxi van to get us close to where my uncle lived.

Traffic in Lagos was chaotic, but driving in Nigeria any given day is chaotic as there is no speed limit. Everyone wants to get places quickly, with drivers often cutting each other off and driving bumper to bumper. Because of the traffic, we had to rush to get our luggage out of the taxi van. We hurried to the sidewalk with all our belongings and hailed yet another taxi that took us to my uncle's house in Ikoyi.

When we arrived at the home in Ikoyi, we were greeted by my uncle's maid and his daughters Val and Shia. Later that day, my cousin Val took me to her father's office to meet him and discuss my return to the United States. I told him that my father had a warrant for his arrest, and that the story about my arrest warrant was a lie. I also told him that my father had fled to the states with my passport and information.

Later that afternoon, when my uncle came home from work, he let me use his cell phone to call my foster mom Mrs. Owillender. It had been so long since I had heard my other mother's voice. After losing my biological mother, I needed some calming comfort and support from the woman who took me in and took care of me as if I was her own.

Even as I dialed the numbers, I began to feel the calmness covering me like a warm blanket being draped around my shoulders. Mrs. Owillender had the softest, sweetest voice. Her voice so often calmed the storm that raged inside me.

I was so excited to hear Mrs. Owillender's voice, and I could tell she was just as relieved and glad to hear my voice as well. She asked me where I was, so I explained to her that my natural father had kidnapped and lured me back to Nigeria with stories about my birth mother. I told her that my mother had passed away in 1999 because of him. She was saddened by this, but she told me to remain strong and she would start the process to get me back home to her in the United States.

She told me that they had had the police looking for me and also that they got some information about my father from my half-sisters and his ex-wife Ruth. They told Mrs. Owillender that my natural father had been planning for a long time to deceive me into trusting him so that he could return me to Nigeria. When Ruth found out he had actually done this thing, she got in contact with Department of Child Services to report him but initially no one believed her. After DCS uncovered more information, they took her claims seriously.

My uncle decided that the first thing we should do was to go to the American Embassy there in Lagos in order to try and obtain a temporary passport. Within a couple of days, one of his drivers took us to the American embassy. The city streets were filled with the unending bustle of people. Nigerian soldiers walked around acting wild with their weapons. The usual people were selling numerous things, from shoeshines to food.

My mind raced as we walked into the American Embassy. I had no identity information or proof of citizenship because my sperm donor took it with him; I hoped they would believe I was a U.S. citizen.

We approached the counter and spoke with a black female working there. It is amazing to me how God watches over you when you don't think of it. All this time I had carried around my wallet without realizing I had an old school ID card inside that would prove that I had come from the United States.

We spent several days gathering as much information as we could, and the embassy workers spoke with my family and caseworkers. After we organized my information and filled out my paper work, we initiated the process of getting a temporary passport. We headed out into the market in search of a photographer who could take a few head shots for my passport. We found a photographer, but his camera was an older film camera rather than a digital one, so the pictures took a couple of days to be developed and printed. I spent my last few days talking to my family in the U.S. and spending quality time with my uncle and my cousins.

After I got my temporary passport, it took about another two weeks to get my plane ticket to return to the United States. My uncle took me to the market in order to buy gifts for my foster parents. He paid for three men's outfits (one for me and two for my foster father) and one outfit for Mrs. Owillender. We also purchased two cans of a powder that we mixed with our tea when I was younger.

A couple of days before I left Nigeria, I was checking an email account that my father had created for me while I was staying with him in New Jersey. I noticed that I had received an email from him stating that would meet me at the airport when I returned to the U.S. and take me back to Nigeria. Luckily the date he had did not correlate with the date on my flight itinerary, because he was one day early.

I probably would have lost my temper if I had seen my father. After reading the disturbing new information, I showed my uncle. As a result, my uncle took more caution to get me on my flight, by having police escorts lead me throughout the airport.

When the day came for me to leave and head back to the United States, I was told at the airport gate that my uncle couldn't go in with me. The airport personnel assured my uncle that I should be fine, and he kept insisting that he go with me, but ultimately they wouldn't let him. So my uncle told me to be safe and call when I could. I headed to my terminal and waited for my section to be called.

As I boarded the plane, I was happy to have spent time with my grandfather and time with my family in Nigeria. I was also happy to be coming back to see my second mother and the family in the United States.

The flight took off and we landed in Amsterdam and then had to switch planes for the long flight over the ocean. This flight was the longest, but I slept through it, and the flight attendants were worried because I slept the majority of the flight. I was simply tired from all the stress and rage I had inside of me.

When the plane landed, I had to go to a different airport for my flight to Salt Lake City. I was on my own until I asked one of the flight attendants where I had to go and she rode with me on the train to the other part of the airport. After she left, I was at the airport for two hours waiting for my flight to Salt Lake City. I sat in the waiting area and then wandered around for a while. As my flight crept closer, I got more and more anxious to finally see my adoptive mother and the rest of the family.

I left Nigeria knowing what a snake my biological father was, and how many women and children he had left behind. I also had anger built up from what my father had done to me, and if I ever saw him again, he would pay the price.

So I set my goals to never be like him. I wanted to be somebody that treated his wife right and someone that took better care of his kids and was always there for them.

Throughout the flight, I had many flashbacks of being in Nigeria. I had many thoughts about my grandpa and what he had to sacrifice in order to get me back here in the United States, and thoughts about my uncle John Ahmadu going out of his way to make sure I got to the United States safely. I had thoughts about hearing the news of my mother passing away and hearing about the terrible things my natural father had done. I also remembered all the times I had with my mother Zipporah by my side.

When the time came, I boarded my final flight back to the states to be with the Lesters. I was glad to be returning to the other person who understood me and was always there for me, as well as the rest of the family. As I walked out of the gate, I saw my adoptive mother with her oxygen tank and the biggest grin on her face because she was so happy to see me. My entire foster family was glad to see me finally be home. I had never been so happy to finally be back and to see my foster parents because of all the sadness I had pent up inside.

On the ride home, my family asked me all sorts of questions and told me that they had the police looking all over for me. They bought me some new clothes and the new Tracy McGrady shoes, because he was one of my favorite athletes at the time.

The next day, family and friends came over to celebrate me coming home. Everyone brought a dish to the get-together, from chicken to barbecued ribs. We celebrated and then I got to spend time with my friends BJ Porter, Mike Thompson, and Mateo Lacey. They told me about the new songs that were out, and which ones were hot and which ones weren't. They also showed me the new dance moves that came out that year.

After a few days, I decided to head back to school. That morning, my sister went to school when the school day actually started and then, with the permission of the school administration, she came back home to pick me up to take me back to school.

I grabbed my school backpack and got in the front seat of our van and we drove to school. When we arrived in the parking lot, the whole student body and all the faculty and staff were outside waiting for me. They applauded me and greeted me upon my return to Layton Christian Academy and the United States. I greeted everyone else back and made my way into the school and into my class.

They were all astonished that I had overcome one of the biggest obstacles of my life.

Chapter 14
Puzzle

AS TIME PROGRESSED, I became acclimated to my new surroundings. The jet lag subsided and I began practicing with the football team, and I also got involved in basketball, soccer and track. Along the way, I was introduced to Sam Russell, the head football coach at Layton Christian Academy.

Coach Russell was a businessman and an investor who started the football program at my high school. He built the coaching staff and funded the project with his own money. He had heard my story and called my adoptive mother to ask if I was going to play football for him. He had no idea that, at the time, I was in a completely different country.

He eventually took me under his wing and taught me the game of football. He told me that football was the only sport that would allow me to use my anger to hit someone legally, but I didn't initially understand what he meant. Coach Russell put me at middle linebacker and started me on some hitting drills. It wasn't until one of the coaches told me to run *through* the ball carrier with everything I had that I understood the concept.

With all that pent up anger and hatred, I exploded into the ball carrier when he came through the hole. He fell back and everyone went crazy, and that was when I felt like I had control and wanted more. I knew then that football and basketball would be what I used to cope with my anger.

Although I was devastated by my biological mother's passing, I started finding strength to hold on and keep moving forward in life. But just as I began to get somewhat comfortable, my adoptive mother's condition began getting worse, and she was admitted to McKay-Dee Hospital. I didn't know how to feel about this, but I never saw her as with someone with an illness. We laughed constantly and talked about my trip being and the things I saw and endured while dealing with my natural father. The bond between us was unbreakable.

Every day after practice, I went to see my mother in the hospital and make her medicine cassette for the fridge. Then we talked for many hours about sports, school, and any troubles I was having.

On May 19th, 2003, I was with Shawn Washington, who was like my brother, just born into the wrong family. His mom's phone rang with a call for me. On the other end was my adoptive father. There was obvious concern in his voice and he was talking softly.

"Son, you have to be strong, ok?" At that moment, it felt like my stomach had dropped to the ground. I had an idea of what he was about to say, but I kept my composure.

"Strong about what?" I asked. His next response brought my whole world crashing down.

"Mom passed away about a couple of hours ago. Her cassette ran out."

I couldn't believe it. I didn't know how to feel or what to believe. Shawn and his mom asked if I was ok and then said they would take me to the hospital right away.

My heart was beating faster and faster as we walked into the hospital because it still hadn't hit me that I had just lost my second mother. After everything that had just occurred, from being kidnapped to finding out my biological mother had passed away, and that my natural father likely had something to do with it, I was in shock. Once we made it to my mother's floor, we walked into her room where she was laying. I said, "mom," but this time she didn't respond.

I couldn't even stay in the room. This was one of the harshest things I had to endure within a short time span. I wanted to commit suicide at that moment. I thought about tossing a chair out the window and jumping out after it. My brothers and my family came to make sure that I was ok because they knew the bond that she and I had.

Losing my adoptive mother was not an easy thing to go through. Life seemed empty and it felt like the important piece of my puzzle went missing. I was sad and I tried crying, but I had no more tears. I had already cried my eyes out after finding out about my biological mother's death. This woman brought so much joy to a boy who had lost faith. As the days passed, I didn't know what to do with myself. I found myself hearing voices in my head every night.

It has hard seeing my mother in that casket the day of the viewing because I hadn't accepted the fact that I had to let her go. I had just begun getting comfortable with Mrs. Owillender. People reassured me that despite the fact that she was no longer with us physically, she would always live with us and around us.

As I sat there during the funeral service, I was still trying to put the pieces together as to why or how this could happen. How could I lose someone who brought back hope to my life that after years of losing my faith? Losing my biological mother was hard enough but this was the dagger that made my heart go numb and cold. I was plagued by questions such as: "What have I done wrong to deserve this? What am I doing wrong?"

After the service, we headed to the gravesite for the burial of the woman who took me in and taught me to never give up and to utilize my gifts. As the small goodbye service came, it began to rain. I gave my sister Mia my suit jacket because she just had her dress on and she was cold. Everyone darted to the vehicles but I stood there for about 20 minutes in the rain just staring at her.

It was a hard pill to swallow. No more late-night talks, no more preparing her medicine, no more hugs, no more anything. I wasn't ready for any of that. As it rained, I glared at the sky and saw comfort in the rain. Every time it rained from that point on, I felt like she was speaking to me.

She had always told me since the day she first came to visit me at my home that I was "always a shining star," no matter what I had been through. After I finally felt comfortable, we headed back to church because there was food and a celebration of the life of my adoptive mother.

Chapter 15
Promises

Mrs. Owillender,

Losing you was one of the hardest things I've had to go through. When you left, life seemed empty. Another important piece of my lifelong puzzle was suddenly missing. Through the sadness and tears, I knew I had to focus on the positive aspects of your life, just to be able to get through mine. My heart slowly started to heal as I reminisced on all the joy you brought to my life. For so many years, I walked around with the weight of the world on my shoulders; this disappointing feeling of not being good enough for anyone. I spent countless days being interviewed for adoption agencies and foster homes because I was unwanted by many. Enduring that struggle made me lose faith in everything I could become. I tormented myself with thoughts of fear and anger.

But those feelings changed when you visited me that lonely day in my temporary home. As you gazed into my eyes, I knew there was something special about you. Who would have known that it was a match made in heaven? You filled missing holes in my heart, just as I filled yours. You picked me up when I was down, and we helped each other along the way. Step for step, we never let each other down.

Thank you for all of the amazing memories we created together. I have fond memories of the days we spent together. My favorite memory is looking over into the bleachers and seeing you support me at my games.

I will never be able to thank you enough for staying strong for me through my darkest days. Thank you for listening to my prayers and being a listening ear when I needed someone to talk to.

God answered my prayers when he brought you into my life. Thank you for being the reason I look up to God and know that I always have a sacred angel above me, blessing my every move. Thank you for giving me the peace of mind that you are no longer fighting a painful battle. I am blessed to know that you are in a new glorious world where you are happy and at peace.

Although your physical presence is no longer with me, you will always live in my heart. As much as I would love to continue to create special memories with you, I know God has a bigger plan for you with Him. After I lost my mother and I found you, it was like finding new motivation. You inspired me to become great, and all I ever wanted was to be as great as you were.

We made several promises to each other that we were determined to keep. So here I am without you, still checking them off my list one by one. I promised you that I would live a life to inspire others, and I will continue to use my broken story to do so. I promised you that I would graduate high school and college; you should have seen me in my cap and gown. I got a high school diploma and a college degree that no one can steal from me. I am still chasing my shot at the NFL, just to show you that I can accomplish everything I set my mind to.

Thank you for being the mom that you didn't have to be.

DeJay

Chapter 16
Liar

THE PASSING OF Mrs. Owillender made our home somewhat quiet. No one knew how to take the loss but we continued our daily tasks and we received support from peers and family. After the passing of my adoptive mother, only my adoptive father, my sister Frantisha, and I, remained. From May through December, we managed to maintain control, but it was hard.

Christmas was never the same given that my adoptive mother was not physically present with us. I could picture her in her grey sweat suit with her oxygen tube in her nose and her tank next to her. It was always a tradition that all the family members come over for Christmas and bring all the nieces and nephews for a family gathering.

That first Christmas, in 2004, all the family was at the house, as was a woman from our church that my adoptive father had invited. My adoptive father pulled my sister Frantisha and I into his bedroom and asked how we felt about the woman. My sister and I thought she was ok, but we wondered why he was asking. He then said he was planning to get married the following year, in February of 2005.

We were shocked by this and we didn't know how to take it. It had not even been a year since our mother passed, and he felt that it was not time for him to get married again. He then came into the living room to make the announcement.

As he made his announcement, everyone became enraged and asked why. My brother Derrick was so enraged he went to his vehicle and left. Then the other family members followed right behind him and took their kids. Our family broke apart and everyone went separate ways.

By this time, my sister was about to head to college, so I would be left to deal with my adoptive father's marriage and my adoptive mother's death alone. As my adoptive father's new fiancée started coming to our home more often, I found myself getting annoyed with her. She came into the home and demanded that we call her "mom." She took some of my mother's

African vases and put water and flowers in them despite the fact that they aren't designed to be used that way.

One day, as she was driving me to school, she was on the phone with one of her co-workers, and she told the co-worker that she was taking her son to school. I looked at her and told her to stop forcing things and stop trying to call me her son. Around the same time, my adoptive father and I started having issues because he felt that he was ready to remarry and I felt he should have waited longer. He figured that we should accept it and try to cope with our loss.

As their wedding day approached, we had more and more problems. I became enraged and annoyed with the whole situation. This new woman thought that she could come into our home and basically put her feet on the couch and be comfortable, which wasn't going to happen. I was supposed to be in the wedding, but because of the issues we were having, I told them take me out of it. I couldn't even bear to do that to my adoptive mother, and especially for a woman that came into my adoptive mother's home and disrespected it and then wanted sympathy and compassion. On their wedding day, I couldn't bear it as I sat in the audience watching. It was another hard pill to swallow.

After the wedding, my adoptive father's new wife came to live with us in our home, and she basically turned my adoptive father against me. Before my sophomore year started at Layton Christian Academy, she had told my father so many lies, including that I was on drugs. They called my coaches and school administrators and took me to the hospital to have blood work done. At the time I had no clue what it was for, but I eventually came to realize that she must have manipulated him to believe that I was on drugs.

My coach Bobby Porter came and told them to stop the madness. I was then placed in Archway Youth Services, a place for youths in drug court or foster care placement, and kids whose parents are abusive or unable to take care of them for a period of time. For whatever reason, my adoptive father believed this woman's lies, and I ended up missing the first week of school as a result of being placed at Archway.

I finally returned to school and started catching up on what I missed from the first week of school. Because this was the year I was supposed to get my driver's license so I could drive to school on my own, my adoptive father and I made a plan for his new wife to pick me up for an appointment at the DMV. I was to be checked out and ready to go by the basketball goals outside. That day, however, I did as I was told and even checked out earlier than I was supposed to. I sat in front near the basketball goals and waited. My school administrator, Mr. Miller, walked by and asked what I was doing. I told him I was about to go get my driver's license. He wished me well and continued walking. After another 20 minutes passed, my basketball coach Bobby Porter walked by and told me to get my butt to class. I laughed and told him that I was headed to get my driver's license. He shouted "Oh man, watch out!" We laughed and he walked away.

As hours passed, I informed my adoptive father that if she didn't make it soon, I would go to football practice. So when 3:30 came, I ran and got ready for football practice. After practice, I saw my adoptive father's Lincoln LS pull up the hill. I asked my coach as he was giving us last-minute reminders if I could go as I was about to go get my drivers license. He gave me permission, so I darted up the hill with my shoulder pads and helmet in each of my hands, still wearing cleats and pads. The trunk was popped open so I threw my stuff in the trunk and shut it. I entered the vehicle behind my adoptive father, who was driving. With excitement, I said, "Can we go?"

"Why weren't you where you were suppose to be?" he demanded.

"What do you mean?" I asked.

"You weren't where you were supposed to be!" he said. I informed him that I waited until 3:30 and then went to practice. I also informed him that I had people who saw me sitting there.

"Are you calling my wife a liar?" he asked.

"Well, no, but I sat there and waited for her and she didn't show up."

"No, you didn't," she said. I told her to stay out of it and to stop lying, and I reminded her that I had witnesses. An altercation broke out between my adoptive father and me, forcing my best friend BJ Porter to run up the hill and pull me away due to the fact he saw I was getting frustrated.

I ended up staying with Coach Porter and his family for about a week. While I was staying there, he and I agreed that it would be best if I stayed with them for the rest of year due to the difficulties at home. Eventually, though, they decided that I would move in with the Millers, my school administrators, for the remainder of my junior year.

The Millers helped my get things back in order and get refocused to finishing high school and playing sports. They became my other family and I was grateful for them helping me when I needed it.

I am so thankful to them for allowing me into their hearts. Family is a big part of every person's life because family supports you, cares about you, loves you and helps you grow into the person you become, and the Millers did that for me. I ended up staying with them until I graduated high school.

I am also grateful to have gone to Layton Christian Academy. If Mrs. Owillender hadn't found LCA, I would likely be hanging out with the wrong crowd and getting into trouble. Perhaps I would have dropped out of school. I am eternally grateful for the Christian example I saw in her, and for the fact that she was always there to encourage and motivate me to do my best.

I also appreciate Coach Porter and the fact that he was always there for me. We talked often about going to college on other people's money. Coach Porter promised my adoptive mother that he would take care of me when she couldn't be there for me and he has kept that promise. I played just about every sport offered at LCA, and excelled in all of them. Sports became my medicine and coping skill.

I arrived at LCA as a kid who struggled with academics and controlling my temper, but with the help of the Millers and others, I transformed my life. Despite the fact that I hadn't been living up to my potential, I ended up graduating with a cumulative 3.2 GPA.

Chapter 17
Rituals

I FINISHED MY senior year well enough to receive a scholarship to Weber State University to play football under Ron McBride, although basketball was my true love.

I had promised my adoptive mother that I would graduate high school and get my degree. We also spoke about being a good person and utilizing my gifts, not just athletically but in being a good person. My biological mother also wanted to see me grow up to be a man of my own, being successful, and being a man she would be forever proud of.

After I signed my letter of intent, I went to Weber State to register for classes and figure out my scholarship situation. Although I was informed that I had a scholarship, when I made it to the registrar's office they informed us that I had a *partial* scholarship. I tried to get in touch with Coach McBride and ask him what was going on. I didn't know anything about the whole process and I didn't really have anyone who could help me understand it, although the Millers and my football coach, Will Hawes, tried.

I never heard anything back from Coach McBride, so I decided to contact Snow College. Snow College gave me a scholarship and I accepted the offer. I signed my letter of intent at my high school and was excited about this new endeavor.

It is one of the enduring rituals of August: Millions of 18-year-olds across the country begin the journey from adolescence to adulthood

After graduating high school, I packed my vehicle with all my belongings and set out on the biggest journey of my life, even given all that I had been through.

The Millers followed me all the way to Ephraim, Utah on the 2-hour drive to the apartment called Snow Village where I going to live with my friend Joseph Sawyer. I had decided to attend Snow College so that Joseph could look after me and so that I would know someone there. Going away to college can be especially scary if you don't know anyone.

Before they headed back, the Millers asked if I had everything. I told them I did, and they said: "Be good and do well." After hugs and goodbyes, they headed back on the 2-hour drive. It was a day filled with great anticipation, emotion, mixed feelings, and, of course, stress.

My freshman year of college was challenging because I was basically on my own and providing for myself. My financial aid and grants covered the majority of my rent, but I still had a portion left to pay on my own. In addition, I had to pay for food and other necessities, so we lived off of ramen noodles and peanut butter and jelly sandwiches. It wasn't a great adjustment, though, because I was used to my biological father not feeding me. We sometimes pitched in together to buy meals for the apartment, and we figured out a way to manage for the rest of the semester.

I began my football career at Snow College as a defensive back and played a great deal as a true freshman on a National Champion-Runner Up team. During my freshman year of football, I learned so much, and football became an outlet for me to express my anger in a positive way. I began to fall in love with all the hard work and preparation for the games. It made me feel like I belonged to a brotherhood that was committed to obtaining a common goal. It also taught me about hard work, and the work that was required in order to get the results that you wanted.

As a result of my upbringing, I knew that I wanted more from life. I wanted to be someone that mattered. I wanted my kids to have everything I never had growing up. So football, in a sense, painted me a picture of where my life could go.

Following my freshman season, I was moved to wide receiver with the foreknowledge that I would need to redshirt based on the depth that was already in place at that position. But I was willing to do whatever it would take to benefit our team. In the 2008 season, I participated on the scout team while redshirting. Many players with my pedigree would have felt that this situation was beneath them, but I wasn't going to let that stop me. I had to stay true to my word because that was all I knew. My work ethic kicked in. While I was on the scout team and learning the offense, I used it as a time to refine my skills as a wide receiver. I also set my focus on improving my life and my situation. While working hard on the field, in the weight room, and in the classroom, my skills improved dramatically. I conducted myself at the highest level and always put the team and program first.

After working hard all through the fall season, Christmas break was upon us. Our last day of school was December 12, which was a Friday. My friend Shawn, and my teammate Cody and I made arrangements to head to Salt Lake City, Utah, for the break weeks in advance. That Friday was just an ordinary Friday. Little did I know my life would change forever.

Chapter 18
Accident

I COULDN'T WAIT to get through my day on December 12, 2008, so I could get back to my room and finish preparing for my future road trip. I finished up my last class and headed back to the room to finish packing.

It was a warm, clear day. The radio was on, the windows were down and I didn't have any worries as I had made the drive numerous times. As we embarked on our road trip down US-89, I had two routes to choose from: I decided to take the course that went through the Spanish Fork Canyon.

About an hour into the drive, we approached an intersection where US-89 turns into US-6 E towards Spanish Fork. My brother and I were discussing whether I was ok to continue driving since I had driven the whole way from Snow College. I assured him once again that I was fine and I told him that if anything changed, I would let him know.

I made a left turn onto the two-lane highway of US-6 E headed toward Salt Lake City. We had about 50 minutes and 52 miles left and it was close to 6 p.m. I was cruising along with Shawn sitting in the front and Cody in the back. The road kept snaking left and right.

Up ahead on the road, we came upon a tan Ford Focus. As we tailed it for a while, Shawn and I noticed that the driver was swerving in and out of the lane and sometimes into the oncoming lane. I kept my distance and continued to keep an eye out for the Focus to ensure our safety.

As we approached the last turn out of the canyons, I remember looking to my left and seeing the field full of big wind turbines. I remember thinking how peaceful that view was and how much I enjoyed this road trip with my brother and my teammate.

I quickly focused back to the road in front of me, remembering that I needed to keep a close eye on the Ford Focus ahead of me. As I turned to face forward, we hit a straightaway that would lead us out of Spanish Fork and onto I-15 northbound toward Salt Lake City. My last memory was of the wind turbines, and then everything went dark. I had no idea what happened or where I was. The only thing I remember was that it was dark all around me and there was a bright light creeping through the darkness. I felt myself falling backwards while trying to grasp the light slowly. The light got darker and darker as I fell. I then opened my eyes and basically came back to life.

For two hours that night, hospital personnel called our friends and family to let them know that the three of us had been in a terrible accident.

As everyone got to the hospital, they found out that my two passengers had minor injuries and mine were the worst. They told my family and friends that a car in front of me lost control and veered into the oncoming lane, hitting a vehicle head-on. A second oncoming driver tried to avoid the wreck and lost control, hitting my vehicle. I then lost control and smacked dead onto the rail on the highway. Shawn and Cody were able to climb out of the vehicle, and when they came to the driver's side to check on me, I was unconscious. I wasn't breathing or moving at all. They tried to wake me up by yelling my name and shaking me and they said my head just fell back. There was blood everywhere: my face was covered in blood and blood was pouring from my mouth. Shawn said he thought he had lost me.

I lost my right central incisor completely and chipped half of the left one. Apparently my head smacked the steering wheel and then the air bag deployed. The ambulance came and rescuers had to use the Jaws of Life to pry my door open so they could drag me out of my vehicle. At this moment, I apparently woke up. My brain had stripped down into the most basic fight-or-flight response and was working on survival mode. I unknowingly fought them as they were trying to get me on the stretcher.

At the hospital, as friends, family, and teammates walked into the hospital room to see me, there were doctors and nurses around me. They cleaned my face and stitched my wounds. They had to remove much glass debris from my face and body. A cast was also made for my left hand as I had fractured it in four places. Some of my friends and family left the room because they couldn't bear to see me like that.

The Millers, however, were there by my side. Friends and teammates from Snow College also came to visit and check on us. They made a get-well poster with candy bars replacing the important words like "crunched," "Butterfinger" and "three musketeers."

"Dear DeJay,

We're sorry ur car got (Crunched bar) and even tho u got some stitches & lost some teeth...ur still (Kissable Hersey Candy)! NEXT TIME u (3 Musketeers) (Butterfinger (better)) BE CAREFUL!!! Because ur worth more than (100 Grand) and like Shawn says, "Ur 2 (Kool) aid pack) TO DIE! Love: Lindee & Morgan."

I didn't remember the sign at all, which is how doctors discovered that I had sustained a mild concussion. When I was released from the hospital, I went home with the Millers and was reunited with Shawn the next day at his grandmother's house.

When I came back to reality, I woke up with the most excruciating pain in my head. My face was hurting and swollen. My face felt stretched. It was difficult for me to talk or smile. My vision was blurry. There was so much pressure in my head that I felt my head was going to explode. I had the worst headache ever. I felt as if someone had a chisel and was continuously chiseling away at my brain.

I couldn't quite pinpoint exactly where I was or whom I was with at the time. I couldn't bear the excruciating pain in my head, so I laid my head back. The Millers drove me to their home and helped me into the house. The next thing I remember was them trying to help me lay down on the bed so I could get some rest. My vision was blurred and I could hardly see straight. My pain was on another level and my head felt pressurized, as if my brain was going to explode.

Every morning for the next two weeks, I would wake up fine, but when I went into the bathroom and saw my face in the mirror, I would come out and ask what happened to me. Shawn had to explain every morning that had happened. I would sit there in shock and think for a minute because I had always told myself that I would never get in an automobile accident. I would look at the pictures of my vehicle and at my scars while I let the reality of what happened soak in.

I went to my appointments when they were scheduled, and I continued my days as normal. A couple of days later, I went out with friends for a birthday celebration. I was determined not to let this minor setback stop me.

The next two weeks were filled with doctor's appointments: chiropractor, urgent care and dentist. I had to get my soft cast changed to a hard one, and I had to set up appointments to get my broken and missing teeth taken care of. In the meantime, I had to wear a retainer with one tooth on it to cover the missing tooth in my mouth.

After days of preparation, my implant surgery occurred in two phases. The first phase was surgical placement of the implant into my gums and bone. My mouth was thoroughly numbed with anesthesia, and an incision was made in my gums to expose the bone underneath. After this incision was made, a specialized drill was used to create space for the implant in the bone. The implant was screwed into place until it was snug, and the gums were closed over the implant.

When I woke up, I could not bear the pain of the surgery. I had the worst headache and I had to be helped into the vehicle. I went home and slept after taking painkillers.

After several months of wearing the implant and the retainer, my mouth began to heal, and I had to go back in for the second phase. The second phase involved making a new incision to expose the implant and screwing a healing cap onto the top of the implant. It helped the surrounding gum tissue to heal. After a few weeks, the healing cap was removed. The abutment then was screwed into the implant and used to support the crown. Eventually, the crown was screwed to the abutment.

Through this tragedy I learned many lessons. To this day, there is nothing like waking up knowing you've been blessed with another day to breathe, to experience life, and to be happy. It is the greatest gift one could receive. I've learned to value life, because I've learned that it could end at any moment. This life we live is unpredictable. While most of us moan over the happenings of our daily lives, we really never stop to think about how a simple act such as walking outside is such a tremendous blessing. It is moments like these that many people take for granted.

My temporary death on that December day frightened me to the core. It takes a long time to work through that kind of personal devastation and, to me, it is ok to take my time recovering. Death became the greatest teacher and the priorities in my life suddenly shifted. The saying, "The trouble is we all think we have time," became so much clearer to me. We need to cherish every moment, for it could be taken away at any given moment. I started approaching life as though there was no tomorrow. Ray Lewis, a linebacker for the Baltimore Ravens, said it best: "If tomorrow wasn't promised, what would you give for today? Forget that there was any sunlight left. What would you spend today thinking about?"

Sometime after the crash, Mrs. Miller recalled the night it happened.

"As a mother, when you get a call late at night, you know it can never be good. We didn't get much information, except that DeJay had been in a car accident and we needed to come right away. My husband and I jumped in the car and started calling everyone we knew to start praying. That was one long hour and half of driving and praying."

"I'd like to say I wasn't worried, but that's just not being honest," she continued. "We didn't know what we were going to find when got to the hospital. Praise God, when we got there, DeJay was awake and fine. He was pretty beat up, and his gorgeous smile had a few teeth missing, but overall we knew he was going to be ok. He had several friends who were already there to check on him, which I'm sure made him feel better."

"The doctor had given him some good medication, so I'm not really sure how much he remembers, let alone who was there," Mrs. Miller recalled. "His recovery went well, but I'm sure it seemed forever to him. We kept reminding him he had to be patient and listen to the doctors and therapists, but it was a very hard time for him. I know he felt like his 'dream career' of playing football was over.

"But again, God is good, as we all can attest today!"

Chapter 19
Grief

GRIEVING THE LOSS of my mother Zipporah, and my adoptive mother Owillender was a very difficult challenge. Mourning my own near death was also a journey without any direction to follow.

It was a lonely journey, no matter how much support I had, because there was so much fear that emerged. I was in a relentless, frightened state, which created scary, hopeless thoughts. These constant thoughts prevented me from feeling lasting connections with others. For a long time after the electrical system of my heart died, I feared that every ache or pain wouldn't be the same. It took a long time to work through that kind of personal devastation and I realized it was ok to take my time recovering.

After my car accident, I discovered that life is too short to not pursue the dreams that are in your heart. I decided that, when it comes to going after what I love in life, I wasn't going to take no for an answer. I started working my butt off so that I could use football as a way out of my situation.

I also had to honor my mothers for all the knowledge they shared with me before God took them to be by His side. In honoring them, I had to remind myself that the best way to honor them was to make my life even better. To pursue the dreams that lie deep in my heart, to invest in people, to live for the small moments, to always remember who I really was, to get my college degree and to never, ever forget how blessed I was. Because all they wanted was for me to be a successful man.

In 2009, I worked hard to become an outstanding player for Snow College, and to be a great leader at my position group. I played with the attitude and toughness that any coach would desire, and I became a full-time starter while maintaining the humility and work ethic necessary to be great. The ultimate goal was to earn a scholarship to a bigger school.

As the season progressed, I received letters and phone calls from different interested schools. On our bye week, during the season, a former teammate of mine and I were invited for a recruiting visit to the University of Wyoming. After our visit, my teammate committed and I informed them I would let them know of my decision soon. I call my family and let them know that I had received my first scholarship to a D1 program, and I asked what their thoughts were.

After conversing with family and friends, I decided to commit to the University of Wyoming because I saw it as an opportunity to get my degree and to continue my football career. I had spoken with other programs prior to committing, but Wyoming offered first and, at the time, seemed like the best fit.

I began the University of Wyoming my junior year. I still had thoughts of losing my mothers, my near-death accident, and all I had overcome to get to where I was, but I was able to use football as a crutch to get out of my situation.

Winter conditioning was no joke. I fought hard but I wasn't getting the playing time I felt I should have. I didn't know anything about transfer rules, so I decided to stick it out my senior year and try to get a starting job.

After fall camp, I was still a 2 on the depth chart. I felt like a failure because I had come to the program to play and not sit out for two whole years. Things were still tough and I lost my fire as a result of not playing very much.

After my senior year, I felt as though I had failed my mission. I believed I had let both my mothers down. I felt like a disappointment, and I felt as though I had some unfinished business with the game of football.

Once I finished my eligibility I began working with troubled youth, but football stayed on my mind 24/7, along with everything I had overcome. I wondered why couldn't I crack this game of football. I started training and contacting arena teams in order to keep pursuing my football career. I was turned away by multiple teams because I didn't have the film that many had. I hadn't played since my sophomore year at Snow College, so I had nothing to show for my playing abilities.

I went to a few 2-a-day waivers with the Utah Blaze, the arena football league located in Salt Lake City, Utah. After being rejected several times, I kept asking myself why I still couldn't crack the code.

I felt as though my career was over and I was a failure. Although I hadn't been playing the game for that long, I had to do something to make myself stick and crack that code.

As 2013 approached, I was invited to play with the Utah Blaze. I felt as though I did well enough to make the team but I had no experience and hadn't learned the arena game yet. After working hard, I received my first ever contract in the Arena Football League. I was excited and felt like this would be a great opportunity to start over again.

After camp, I was released, and I once again felt disappointed. I didn't know what to do, so I spent many hours wondering what I could do better. I focused on working and helping the kids.

One day, I received a text message from a former Wyoming teammate, Tashaun Gibson, who was playing for the Cleveland Browns at the time. He gave my info to a guy named Scott Porter who would help me to get in contact with some other arena teams.

After speaking with Scott porter, we decided that that the Green Bay Blizzard would be the best opportunity for me to get my feet wet. I spoke with Chad Baldwin, the head coach at the time, and shared little about my story and background. He was excited to give me an opportunity, although it would only be for the last two games of the season.

He also asked me to share a portion of my story with the team, which was by far was one of the hardest things I had ever done, looking back on the situation. After hearing my story, the other players looked at their own situations and were thankful they didn't have it worse.

Once game day came, it was now or never. I felt as though I had to seize the moment and opportunity. I came out and did what I had to do in the last two games of the season. After the season, I was planning on heading back to Salt Lake City to work with the troubled youth, until I received a phone call from the Utah Blaze.

I signed a contract with them and, though I had never ever played arena football before, I took advantage of the opportunity. My first play in arena football came in the second half after playing special teams the whole game. I ran a corner route for a touchdown and slammed hard into the wall. It was the most amazing feeling ever. I felt as though things had begun to shift and go in the right direction. I took advantage of the last four games of the season with the Utah Blaze to start what I called unfinished business.

Chapter 20
Lessons

FOR THE LAST few years, I have spent my time playing professional football for the Arena Football League. I have broken barriers and overcome so many obstacles to get where I am now. More importantly, I was able to use the game of football as leverage and motivation to obtain my college degree, just like I promised my mother I would. My dream is to continue climbing the ranks through the higher levels of football.

If my dream ends here, though, I would be content with how far I have made it. In comparison to where I came from I am pleased with where I am now. Looking back, I realize that hard work and goal setting allow anyone to accomplish anything he sets his mind to.

To the game of football, I simply want to say thank you for shaping me into the man I am today. You have taught me so many valuable keys and skills that I will carry with me for the rest of my life. First, you taught be the value of hard work: from waking up every day and going to practice, to the extremely painful sacrifices my body made for this game. Although it wasn't always a beautiful luxury, you taught me that hard work will get you noticed. Hard work helps me accomplish my goals in life.

Next, you taught me how to be prepared. I've learned that preparation is key to being successful and preparation leads to spectacular results and winning games. I have summed the importance of preparation into 6 p's: Proper preparation prevents piss poor performance.

Lastly, I have learned the lifelong measure of dedication. I dedicated myself to this game even if I did not know where it would lead me. Turns out that my dedication to football has taught me that I have the courage to dedicate myself to other things in my day-to-day life. Football has taught me that the game is like life. Just like football, life requires hard work, perseverance, sacrifices, and dedication.

Most importantly, it has taught me to keep my head up when odds are stacked against me. Without these key skills, I wouldn't be as successful as I am today.

I have learned a little something about the game of football throughout my past years that I continue to apply to the game today. The game of football will squeeze the blood, sweat and tears out of a person while turning your dreams into reality. At times, you will be faced with setback after setback, and you learn to take a step back and reconfigure yourself so you can be successful.

Your thought process and how you approach this game will determine how successful you will become. As a player, there are so many people who live vicariously through you. The best feelings in the world are created by experiences you have through football, and some of those feelings are hard to duplicate. The feeling of long bus rides with the team, the bruises all over my body, and my pre-game routines are hard to beat. You have to be focused on the task at hand in this game; you have to focus on the plays, the game, and the faceless opponent.

You grow to realize that your football team is your family; they have your number when your back is against the wall. You mess with one player, you've got us all. Life is a team game; in other words, life is the big game.

Along this football journey, I was given the greatest gift anyone could ask for: the birth of my beautiful daughter. No words can describe the way it felt holding her for the first time. The feeling I have while holding that little girl is unlike anything I have ever felt. I absolutely wouldn't trade it for anything in the world. She makes me feel like I am bigger than life. She already has me wrapped around her finger, and she is the center of my whole world. She had the ability to bring joy to my life and my heart belongs to that sweet little girl.

My promise is to be the best father I can be to my daughter. I want her to grow up having the support of a loving father as her role model. I feel as though there are certain milestones a father, and parents in general, should be present for throughout their child's life: things such as graduations, sports, and school functions. As she gets older, my goal is to make it to every event she is participating in. Also, I want to prove to her that she has a father who cares for her more than anything. I want to be able to provide her with anything she can imagine. I want to comfort her when she cries, be her listening ear when she has secrets to tell, and her support system when she needs me. I will be here every step of the way as she finds her place in this world.

To this day, I still have my fair share of struggles, but I continue to keep pushing and moving forward. Life gets rocky at times, but I have found the strength to keep loving and living. I have learned from experience that life is not a game for wimps. Don't resist your suffering. At our lowest points, we have the tendency to unattach ourselves from things and people so we stop getting hurt.

A word of advice: the longer we allow ourselves to chase fame, recognition, money or other materialistic items, the longer we will feel as though we are suffering. Society leads us to feel like we need those things to live a proper life, and that is simply not true. To be remarkable in America, people believe that we have to always one-up our peers. That is our egos in competition with others. Let go of the life you want to live and live the life you have right now.

Don't allow your mind to overpower the kindness in your heart. Our minds create stories to dwell on. Stories are not always our real experiences. What you believe and how you believe affects the life you live.

Chapter 21
Discovery

FINDING YOURSELF IS the greatest discovery, but it takes a lot of time; years, in some cases. We do not know who we are and what we aspire to be unless we evaluate the plus and minus in our character, the way and means of removing our faults and the steps to be followed to try for refinement. There have been many discoveries so far but finding yourself is the toughest of all. It requires perseverance, calm and clear thinking, and a crystal clear mind to find yourself. James Thurber says "all men should strive to learn before they die what they are running from and to and why." This is the gist of life and enlightenment.

The year I was about to turn 23, I realized that I would be going into the working world and starting the second chapter in my life, so I decided to write words of encouragement for the younger me. As part of that process of introspection, I found myself wishing I had a father in my life. I realize that I was blessed to have great father figures in OD Lester and Sam Russell. I decided to give myself the advice I didn't have the ears to hear 23 years ago. From that exercise, I came up with a list of things I learned the hard way, and I hope that it serves to help some young man in his path to manhood and in his path to pursue success.

It's common to seek the approval of others, which can lead you down the path of doing things just because others want you to. It isn't so common to follow your heart and believe in yourself. Learn to love the person that you are and not who others would have you be.

Remember that happiness is the key to value. Enjoy your life as much as you can and make the best out of every situation. If you are truly happy, then other people won't be able to bring you down with their judgments.

Finding happiness is the definition of success in life. Realize that you are your own person and ultimately the only one in charge of your own actions and feelings. You cannot control other people, but you can control how you react and feel about them. Be yourself! Life is simply not fun if you are so worried about pleasing or offending other people that you can't even have a personality! Truth is, not everyone is going to like you anyway, so why bother trying? Let them get mad over petty stuff if they want to, but don't become a victim of that kind of stupidity and small-mindedness. Just have fun. But don't be afraid to be yourself. Don't change yourself just because someone wants you to or because they are judging you. You are you, and you can't be anyone different. Understanding that you matter goes a long way, because you start doing things for "YOU."

Also, learn to laugh at yourself; it's an important skill to have. If we're so hung up on always being right, or always winning, or always being "perfect," we'll miss out on a lot of life. Making mistakes is how we learn, and the more comfortable we are with failing, the less afraid we are to take chances. Love who you are, not who you think you ought to be.

All of us are born with something special to share with the world. Don't listen to those who would tell you otherwise. You count. You're amazing. You're perfect just as you are. Don't try to be someone else, and don't try to be something for someone else. Follow your own counsel always, and trust your heart.

When you look at yourself in the mirror, you want to be proud of yourself and the choices you've made. That won't be the case if you're not brutally honest with yourself. A true man takes the consequences of his actions and doesn't try to get out of them or pretend they didn't happen. If you make a mistake, admit it and make it right. You'll always have to answer to the man in the mirror, so do yourself a favor and do right the first time.

Lastly, stop comparing your life to others' lives. Everyone's journey is different. I know everyone is afraid that they are not good enough in some context, which gets them in trouble. You can't let people shake you or make you go your whole life trying to please everyone else, whether it's your hair, your clothes, your words, your feelings, your beliefs or your possessions. Other people's judgment of you should never stop you from being YOU!. When you let their judgment dictate who you are, you are no longer your own individual, but someone that everyone else wants you to be.

When someone posts something on social media telling us we're not popping unless we have that item or because were not on a vacation to Vegas like they are, it's easy to feel like you're not good enough. But that's not the way to live. Society has made us live in an endless cycle that keeps repeating itself. When you take the bus, for instance, people make fun of you and say you don't have a car, but when you get a car, they belittle it because it's not a Porsche. It just never ends because you can never be good enough according to everyone else's opinion.

Never give up on your dreams.

People will always try to tell you what you should do with your life, mostly based on what they want from you. Sometimes it's based on what they wish they had done or what they did do, and sometimes they simply want to live vicariously through you. But at the same time, remember that you're the one who will have to live with those decisions, so if you are being pushed to go to college, and all you want to do is draw or paint, don't let others decide for you.

Not everyone needs to go to college, be a professional athlete, be a doctor, etc. If your heart tells you to play guitar and write music all day, then getting a degree in accounting isn't going to be fulfilling to you. Listen to your heart. There are many successful people in the news that didn't graduate college who are making it in life. Steve Jobs was a college dropout. My high school coach quit the first day of college and now owns multiple car dealerships. Michael Jordan was cut from his high school basketball team and he took it upon himself to never give up on his dream of playing basketball. He is now one of the all-time greats to ever play the game of basketball.

If you want something in life, go out and get it. Period. No ifs, ands, or buts. Because, in this game of life, easy is not an option. It's always going to be hard striving for your dreams, but dreams are possible. As we look into the world, many people have fulfilled their dreams, so why can't we all? I've learned over the years that regardless of your circumstances, you must embrace faith. With faith, anything is possible.

Don't ever let anyone hold you back. If you allow others to define your dreams and abilities, then you enable them to hold you back. What you're capable of achieving is not a based upon what other people think is possible for you. What you're capable of achieving depends on what you choose to do with your time and energy. Life is an open-ended journey and what you achieve comes from what you want to achieve as long as you are willing to put forth the time and effort to achieve it.

Last, and I think mostly importantly, you need to apply discipline and consistency. Most people want handouts and are not willing to put in the work to attain their dreams or goals. Everyone wants a perfect body. They go to the gym several times and call it quits because they are not willing to apply the discipline and consistency to keep going to the gym day in and day out. You have to be willing to treat every minute of every day as an opportunity to get better. Going to the gym is about productivity. What you do in the gym is what counts, and it can be transferred to life and to your dreams.

Be a good parent.

I know how hard it was to grow up without a father, and I am constantly reminded of some of the things I couldn't' do because my father was not there to teach me. We need our fathers to teach us confidence, self-esteem, strength and leadership. Although mothers are perfectly capable of this, there is no substitute for two different perspectives. As a kid, you need both sides, so you can better understand the world.

As a child, I felt like I was deprived of something so important. Why me? I felt loneliness, sadness, envy, and the list goes on.

But that's not the end. I was raised without a major male influence in my life, meaning I had to bear the brunt of lessons in the school of hard knocks. But that has made me a stronger and more intelligent person in life. So don't fret and don't be upset. Just live your life. Because while there is no substitute for a parent, there is also no better teacher than learning all you know by yourself.

I know that, because of what I went through, no child of mine will ever be alone. Which means that my experience will have been for the best.

The musical group Jagged Edge said it well in their song No Respect.

"I respect a man raisin his kids all on his own,
I respect a man who makes sure he takes care of home,
you gotta respect a man with good judgment,
cuz I'll be damned if someone's taking care of my kids
and I respect a man who treats his woman like a queen,
I know you're not perfect you ain't gotta be so mean,
no matter how strong she is for a woman,
a man should never attempt to lay his hands on her.
There's more to life than what happens on your block,
just treat your women right and hold 'em at the top,
gotta raise these kids and teach 'em, never don't ya stop,
you ain't no man to me if you let your family starve,
got no respect for them dudes who hit they women and,
got no respect for the fools who leave they children and
I just wanna take care of my family
got no respect if you ain't trying to do the right thing"
(Jagged Edge).

My ordeal with my natural father has taught me valuable lessons that I will carry forward in my life. It has taught me to never abandon my child or to do anything to hinder that bond. Raising kids is a complicated endeavor, and there's no one recipe for doing it right. But I just hope and pray that I can bestow the love my mother bestowed upon me to my newborn daughter, Olivia.

Embrace the struggle.

There's no real way to pretend things never happened because we are here to learn and cope. We don't always understand the reason things occur. Just like the moon comes out at night and the sun comes out during the day, sometimes bad things do happen to good people and you must embrace it.

Hang in there, because everything is going to be alright. It may not happen when you expect it, but eventually it will. I've learned that you can embrace the struggle and use it as an opportunity to become stronger and more resilient, or you can let it break you.

One of my all-time favorite movies growing up was The Lion King. Rafiki said it best when he said, "The past can hurt. But the way I see it, you can either run from it, or learn from it."

Most people run away from it as if it will make the situation go away, but it is through pain and struggle that we tend to experience growth. Those who stick around to learn from it are the ones becoming successful and accomplishing greater things.

Also understand that you shouldn't go back to the past because it's not who you are anymore. You need to use it as fuel for how you will fight for your future.

Many people search endlessly for a magical formula for success. They don't realize that successful people are the ones who embraced the struggle and learned from it. They didn't use it as a crutch, but as a fuel to want more, be more and do more. The struggle is going to be one of the biggest fights of your life.

Fighting teaches you strength and courage to take on whatever is coming your way in the future. When you decide not to fight or embrace the struggle, you take the path many people take every day: letting fear, the past, and all the bad experiences, take over. This leads to them being content with being average, and taking things as they are without having the desire to want more from their lives.

Finally, understand that hard times are sometimes blessings in disguise. No matter what wounded you, hurt you, or made you bleed, keep your head up. No matter how much its hurts you, keep a smile on your face and keep pushing forward by taking it one day at a time.

Forgive and grow.

Forgiveness is a process, and it is a difficult thing to do. Being able to forgive someone who cut you is one of the most powerful tools you can have in this game of life. That's why I've learned to not hold grudges and to smile at everything. It doesn't matter if it's a relationship, job, or lifestyle, if it doesn't make you happy or is bringing you down, let it go. It's like finding yourself in a wrong story. Why keep tormenting yourself? It doesn't make sense.

For years I struggled with anger from all I have been through. I always asked myself "Why me?" But once I learned about forgiveness and forgave those in my past who did me wrong like my father, I began to let the situation just be what it is. No looking back, no trying to make sense of it, no looking for overdue apologies or explanations but most importantly just accepting that it occurred and utilizing all the lessons it has taught me so that I can move on with my life. I couldn't bear to carry all the negative energy, guilt, resentment, and pent-up frustration because it started to affect my overall health. It was not an easy process but I stuck with it and made it happen, because everything that happens to us is there to teach us something about growing as a person.

I believe that monsters come in all shapes and sizes, and sometimes they are the people we care most about in this world. When we learn to forgive and grow, it helps us heal internally. It takes a lot of courage to forgive people who hurt you or people who walked out on you.

It has been said that, "where we are headed is more important than where we've been; that's why the front windshield is bigger than the rear view mirror." I believe that completely because it has been true for me. I had to have faith that where I was headed was way more important than where I came from. I made up in my mind that wherever I was headed wasn't going to be where I would spend all my life.

Be willing to fail.

You need to understand that you're going to make mistakes. But make it the best mistake. We learn through trial and error. You can't get to where you want to be in life if you don't fail at something; and the fact that you fail doesn't mean you're a failure. The path to success, or wherever you set your goal to, won't be easy. Your will and faith will be tested time after time. If you never have faith that you'll get where you want to be then things won't work out in your favor. Before they even begin to work, you will already have given up. Life itself will present many challenges and obstacles, but that's what makes the end result worth it.

The three hardest lessons most people will encounter in life are heartbreaks, financial struggles and failures. When these things occur, you have to be willing to keep moving forward and find ways to keep surviving the day. But in order to survive those days, you have to be willing to grind and make moves. Do your best and when you do that, you will get where you're meant to go.

Don't take things for granted

Understand that this will be a hard lesson to learn, but it will be the most important lesson. Life can change in an instant. Make sure you appreciate what you have, while you still have it. When I was younger, I always thought my parents were going to be there forever and that nothing could go wrong. I learned the hard way that they won't always be there. The way I lost my mother was hurtful. I never envisioned living life without my mother at such a young age. My mother had taught me everything she could and more but the one thing she never taught me was how to live life without her. It hurt me tremendously and I didn't know how to deal with the situation.

Most people don't appreciate what they have until it's gone: family, friends, health, job, and money. They don't appreciate it because they believe that it will be there tomorrow, which is not necessarily the case. Nothing in your life is guaranteed to be there tomorrow, including loved ones.

If you think you have plenty of time to get back in touch with your old friends or spend time with new ones, you don't. You think you have the money to spend, or you think you'll have it next month, but you might not. So start embracing and appreciating the little things before life teaches you the lesson by taking something you so dearly love away.

Have no regrets.

Don't settle.

And never, ever forget how truly big we are blessed.

When it comes to going after what you love in life, don't take no for an answer.

Priorities in life suddenly shift. Death can be one of our greatest teachers.

Chapter 22
Encouragement

DeJay,

Keep working hard and stay focused on the long game and not just the short game. I have watched your posts and messages and had a couple of thoughts that I hope will encourage you.

Everyone knows the saying stay focused on what's important. The trouble is we all sometimes have difficulty knowing what is really important. There is a whole lot of life ahead of you. Enjoy the current moments, follow your passion and your heart, but keep in mind that some of the things that are important to you now will not be in 15-20 years. Keep in mind that you have a whole life ahead of you, and make sure to plan for that life.

I know having a great family is important to you, so keep building yourself and your life so that you are ready to be the best husband and dad you can be. You have been gifted physically and are great at football, but keep in mind that you have gifts and abilities that go beyond physical and go beyond football. Make sure you cultivate those gifts and abilities also. Keep your eye out for possible opportunities and careers that you can do for a lifetime that you can be passionate about and excel in.

I saw your post about finding new friends. I think this is part of growing up. A lot of times we grow at different rates than our current friends. It is not always our fault or their fault; it just happens in life. You are right to look for those who are on the same path that you are: friends that can help you with your growth and friends that you can help with theirs. I heard once that the world is full of Friends, Foes and Fools. Learning to tell the difference is not always easy.

Keep working hard, and keep focusing on the long game. When obstacles and roadblocks come your way, find ways over, around and through them. Not allowing yourself to be discouraged is one of the best skills you can develop in life. Whether you reach all of your goals or not, keep working toward them. Many times the preparation and work that we put in for our goals equip us for something other than our original goal. The bottom line is doing the right thing, working hard and sticking to it is always its own reward.

I am proud of you and what you have accomplished and I look forward to your successes both soon and in the future. You have come a long way; keep your eye on the long game.

-Mr. Miller

DeJay was a 7th grader in my first math class at Layton Christian Academy. I didn't know his story at the time, but I could tell there was more behind what I saw initially. I saw a boy that just wanted love and acceptance but instead tended to act out, go against the grain and test the waters. We had plenty of discussions about what was acceptable and what was not. He was a smart kid, but he seemed to be distracted with life, and I had a hard time getting him to get his work done.

Although he struggled in the classroom to stay on task, the basketball court was a different story. I've never seen the talent in junior high that I saw in him. It was literally like he was four years older than everyone else. I remember watching him play basketball and being amazed by his speed. He was so fast at running. One play, he stole the ball and ran full-speed down the court leaving everyone in his dust. When he got to the other end, however, he was running so fast he couldn't stop to shoot the basketball. He just threw it up as he ran past it. He didn't make the shot, but the speed he showed was incredible. It didn't matter that he didn't make the shot because he did make 99% of the other ones.

As the years passed, we learned more about DJ's past. It broke my heart to think that a child had to endure what he did, and given the circumstances, I understood why he struggled. He had an anger problem, and I'm sure it was due to his situation.

I remember he was playing basketball at lunch and he got mad at another student and threw the ball at his head in such anger. Once again, we had a very stern talk at that time about appropriate behavior.

It required constant guiding, but I started to see this amazing change in this child. I could see God's love making His way into his heart. Each year he got more controlled and mature. He found ways of handling his anger and not being the victim but a survivor. In high school, he really started to mature and take control of his own life, regardless of the adults' decisions around him. He became stronger, more confident and a pure example of perseverance.

I don't remember if it was his sophomore or junior year, but when he was abandoned in Africa, we could hardly believe our ears. DeJay had come so far and matured so much and now he was facing another setback. How much did one child have to go through in his very short lifetime? Everyone prayed for DeJay and we kept constant tabs on what was happening and how long it would be before we could get him back. We celebrated when we eventually got him back! We worried, however, about how this would affect DJ in the long run. Once again, he showed his strength and made lemonade out of lemons. He is truly amazing.

He has now graduated from college and is playing football professionally and is a pure example of strong, incredible young man. Whenever I see him, he gives me a big hug and it is like my son has come home. He holds such a special place in so many hearts. I loved seeing his positive posts on Facebook and always seeing the light in situations that might get you down. Lord knows he has had plenty of practice in this field.

I couldn't be more proud of him and can't wait to see what God has in store for him in the future. I know God will use those trials to use DeJay in a big way!

-Mrs. Elmy

I first met DeJay Yusef Mamman in December, 1998. I was sitting in my office at the Clearfield Job Corp as the Residential Living Manager. I heard a knock on my door and Dr. Joseph Mamman entered along with his two sons. Dr. Mamman was a counselor in the Residential Living department who would stop by from time to time. I noticed DeJay because his bright big eyes were focused on my candy dish. I laughed and asked if he and his brother would like some candy, and they quickly helped themselves. I did not know that our paths would cross again and I would watch this boy grow into a man. Faith would have it that he and my son would be best friends and I would have a chance to coach and mentor him.

When my good friends the Lesters talked to me about bringing their daughter and new adopted son to LCA, I was pleased. I had left the Clearfield Job Corp and was now the Director of Students and head Varsity Basketball Coach at Layton Christian Academy. I found out the young man they were so excited about was DeJay Yusef Mamman, the young man I had met two years earlier in my office at the Job Corps center. DeJay had those same big bright eyes and he listened carefully to every word that we adults were saying.

DeJay Yusef Mamman, who later changed his name to DeJay Yusuf Lester, worked hard to have an incredible athletic career and also contributed greatly to the everyday life of the Students at LCA. He was one of the captains of the football team, the basketball team (2007 State Champions) and soccer team, and he was chosen Homecoming King his senior year. DeJay graduated from LCA a true renaissance man!

-Bobby
Porter

It was 2003, and I had just been asked to be the first head coach of the new football program at Layton Christian Academy. I remember asking the athletic director, Coach Porter, to compile a list of potential players. The list was short; almost too short for a football team.

I began calling players to inform them of our first practice date. One of the players was DeJay Lester. His mother answered

117

the phone only to tell me DeJay was on vacation and would be back in a week or so. Throughout the first week of practice, I kept hearing about this exceptional athlete that would soon join the team. It was during one of those practices that I learned that DeJay had been kidnapped.

I first met DeJay at his homecoming after he was returned to Utah. It didn't take long for me to notice that DeJay was, in fact, an exceptional athlete, but he was also angry and untrusting. It wasn't until I got to know him better that I understood why.

Over the next 4 years, DeJay and I formed a bond that was both strong and heartfelt. Our relationship continued as DeJay moved on to college football, and it still continues to this day. DeJay is like a son to my wife and me. His story is remarkable and yet he remains grounded in his Christian beliefs and his life. Maybe it's because of his Christian beliefs that he is grounded.

Coach
Samuel
H.
Russell

Made in the USA
Columbia, SC
23 June 2017